# Open My Eyes, Lord

## A Practical Guide To Angelic Visitations And Heavenly Experiences

# Open My Eyes, Lord

**A Practical Guide To Angelic Visitations
And Heavenly Experiences**

# GARY OATES

*with*

# Robert Paul Lamb

**Open Heaven Publications**
*an outreach of Gary Oates Ministries, Inc.*
P.O. Box 457/Moravian Falls, NC 28654 USA
336-667-2333
www.GaryOates.com

**Seventh Printing—October 2013**

Unless otherwise noted, all Scripture quotations are from the NEW AMERICAN STANDARD BIBLE (R), Copyright (c) 1960, 1962, 1963, 1968, 1971, 1972, 1973, 1975, 1977, 1995 by The Lockman Foundation. Used by permission.

## Open My Eyes, Lord

Requests for information should be directed to:

### Open Heaven Publications
*an outreach of Gary Oates Ministries, Inc.*
P.O. Box 457/Moravian Falls, NC 28654 USA
336-667-2333
www.GaryOates.com

Printed in the United States of America

# Dedication

To my beautiful wife, Kathi, who has stood with me through "thick and thin", my partner, my co-laborer, and my best friend

and

To my parents, Harmon & Ruby Oates, who have gone to be with the Lord...for all the years of encouragement, support and especially for their ceaseless prayers.

*Then Elisha prayed and said, "O Lord, I pray, open his eyes that he may see."* *And the Lord opened the servant's eyes and he* saw; and behold, the mountain was full of horses and chariots of fire all around Elisha.

2 Kings 6:17

# *Acknowledgements*

Randy Clark—for believing in me and giving me an opportunity to touch the nations of the earth, and also for his many prayers of impartation.

Heidi Baker—for inspiring me to become a passionate lover of God.

Henry Madava—for allowing the Holy Spirit to work through him which powerfully impacted my life.

Mike Shea—for opening up the Scriptures regarding Romans 6:13 which has been a key to the remarkable events that have occurred in my life.

Robert Paul Lamb—my long time friend who tirelessly helped me in so many different ways to bring this book into reality. Thank you for your expertise in writing and especially for your heart to diligently seek God during the whole process.

# *Endorsements*

Gary Oates' new book, *Open My Eyes, Lord,* is captivating, in the fullest sense of the word. While it is theologically sound, it is also experientially riveting.

This is a story that is not content to remain on the pages of a book. It contains the very heart of God, igniting everything it touches. Somehow the story of Gary's encounters with the Lord has affected my own hunger for God.

Reader beware, this quest is contagious!

Bill Johnson, Pastor
Bethel Church
Author, *When Heaven Invades Earth*

This is the first book I have ever read that shows you in practical steps how to achieve intimacy with the living God.

Gary Oates, not only provokes you to jealousy by his supernatural walk with God, but he also encourages you to walk in this special intimacy.

Sid Roth
TV & Radio Host
Messianic Vision

I could not put down this amazing book! I laughed and cried as the Holy Spirit touched me through these anointed stories. If you want a deeper life in the Holy Spirit, this book is for you! The stories of angelic encounters will have you hungry for your own. You will be blessed.

Heidi Gayle Baker, Ph.D.
Director, Iris Ministries
Co-Author, *There's Always Enough*

I was handed the manuscript to this book on a recent Sunday afternoon on my way home to Florida. I promised Gary that I would try to look at it within the next few days. I started browsing it upon retiring that night. I was riveted to the pages and was through page sixty-five before I slept. I finished it the next day.

Many things blessed me but the Scriptural study of the ministry of angels brought me to tears. It wasn't all new but—in the midst of my grief over the loss of my wife less than ninety days before—I had all but forgotten the precious ministry of angels. That night through a simple recognition of their availability, I received the comfort of their presence. Thank you, Gary, for letting us in on your ongoing experiences in the normally unseen realm!

Jack R. Taylor
President, Dimensions Ministries
Melbourne, Florida

If you are looking for a book that will usher you into God's presence—this is it! *Open My Eyes, Lord* reveals the passion and experience of Gary Oates who sees into the invisible realm. This has resulted in natural "supernatural" living.

When I read a book, I look for the life of the Lord in experience and expression through the author. Gary Oates' testimony has brought me to my knees with a desperate cry, "Open My Eyes, Lord."

Leif Hetland
President, Global Mission Awareness
International Conference Speaker


Since the time of Revelation 4:1 (when the Lord spoke to the apostle John, *"Come up here, and I will show you what must take place..."*), the Church has had an invitation to come up higher and deeper into the Spirit realm. Gary Oates is opening the way—in this book—for many to do this very thing.

*Open My Eyes, Lord* was exciting to read, and made me hunger for more of the spiritual realm. God is truly opening our eyes in this special season. Thanks, Gary, for being willing to go beyond your comfort zone into the unknown adventures of the heavenly realm.

Michael Ellis
Nehemiah Ministries
Kennesaw, Georgia

This book opens the eyes and ears of a true child of God in a most wonderful way. While captivating the reader, it brings a feeling of the awesomeness of God. It also brings boldness in the presence of the supernatural. The result is a greater hunger for God. I recommend both leaders and lay people read this book.

Henry Madava
Pastor, Victory Church
Kiev, Ukraine


I met Gary & Kathi on the Global Awakening ministry trip to Volta Redonda mentioned in the book. It was my great joy to see how the Holy Spirit "opened their eyes" to see the invisible realities that our faith speaks of. Gary's simple and straight-forward testimony is refreshing from someone who is in ministry.

I would like to encourage you: let his testimony build your faith. Not only have I been with them since their life-changing experience to see its good fruit, I have witnessed as the Holy Spirit has done the same in the lives of others. Indeed we are coming to a time in which we will have many "seers" within the Church. My prayer is: May the Lord open your eyes too!

Michael Shea
Casa de Davi
Londrina, Brazil

# Table of Contents

# Foreword

*Open My Eyes, Lord,* Gary Oates' new book, is one of the most exciting books I have read in a long time. It is a book about holiness and intimacy with our Triune God; Father, Son and Holy Spirit.

Gary's pursuit of a life of intimacy with God and consecration to a lifestyle of holiness has been shared with his wife, Kathi. However, their walk with God took a gigantic leap forward after Gary saw the Lord Jesus while out of his body, and both he and Kathi's eyes were also opened to see angels.

Gary's story is very unusual, and I am sure that there are some who will find it difficult to accept, but I was there when all these things happened to him. I was standing beside him in Volta Redonda, Brazil when the initial experience occurred.

I remember seeing him and thinking something is going on with Gary. He's in a trance or he's had an experience. I remember seeing his body fly back, knocking down several rows of chairs, and almost knocking over a pastor when Gary's spirit came back into his body.

I remember seeing him lying on the floor shaking with tears gushing from his eyes. I can verify this story. I am a witness to what Gary has written and more. He hasn't told all his experiences of seeing into the spiritual realm.

You may believe that I too am gullible and that we both have been deceived. Let me tell you why I believe Gary's story. We were in Manaus, Brazil in 2003 ministering in Apostle Rene Terra Nova's church—a congregation of 48,000 members. The huge sanctuary seats 10,000.

We had been there for almost a week, and had been praying for the sick always using the same modus operandi, having the ones who had ex-perienced at least eighty percent healing to wave both hands over their heads. However, ninety percent reported healing on the last night of services.

What was the difference on this last night?

This was the night that Gary told me about seeing warrior angels. It was also the night that Gary saw whirlwinds of fire come into the room over people's heads. The only difference—I am able to determine—between 9,000 healings this night and perhaps 500 or so healings the other nights was the reported presence of the warrior angels and the healing angels.

If Gary had told me what he saw and there had been no significant difference in the number of healings, then I would have had difficulty believing what he thought he was seeing. But in this case, he told me *in advance*—before the explosion of healings. Thus, the most logical explanation for me is that he is really seeing into the spiritual realm.

Perhaps it is easier for me to accept Gary's story because it brings me back to my spiritual roots. One of the most important spiritual events in my family as a child was my mother's experience of being taken out of her body and her spirit going into heaven. This happened when I was about six years old.

My dad was backslidden at the time, and mom was so touched that for days she was in a trance-like state muttering, "It was so beautiful, it was so peaceful, I don't want to stay here. I want to go back."

This shook my dad. He would tell mom, "You must stay here. We have three small children, and I need you." But, mom would just cry, overwhelmed by the wonder of the glory of the experience, and walk off saying, "I want to go back." For over forty years, my mother was unable to talk about this experience without weeping.

I was raised in a Baptist home and attended a Baptist college and later The Southern Baptist Theological Seminary. Though raised as a Baptist, I believed that conservative evangelicals have experiences with God that are very supernatural. I met too many Baptists who had such experiences before I ever met a Pentecostal or Charismatic.

While majoring in religion at a Baptist college, I did a term paper on out of body experiences. In the process I went back to my hometown and interviewed three other people who had similar experiences as my mother.

One of those interviewees was Carlton Brockett, a deacon in the General Baptist church my family attended. I read the letter he wrote home during World War II about his experience of having seen heaven open up to him. This was a most spiritual man who also couldn't talk about his experience—even decades later—without being moved to tears.

Then, there was his sister, Hazel Phelps, another General Baptist, who was taken out of her body while doing housework. During her experience, she was told that her husband, who she had been praying for over twenty years, would be saved. Without saying anything to anyone, he went to church that night with her and gave his life to Jesus.

During this research I met two men who had seen my mother fall to the ground when she was taken to heaven. She was leaving a house on the way to her car and got as far as the sidewalk. The two men told me they could not get a pulse and there was no sign of breathing. They also said her body became cold, and that she was gone for a matter of minutes. By the time of my interview—some sixteen years after mom's experience—both of these men had become ministers of the Gospel.

I thank God that my family had its own stories of the reality of the spiritual world. Our Christianity wasn't just related to truths from the ancient past, but instead was a Christianity where the realities of the Bible were still possibilities in our lives.

My grandmother had heard the audible voice of God tell her to go into a bedroom and she would be healed. She obeyed, went into the bedroom, began to pray, and a large goiter on her body disappeared. She told me as a small boy, "It felt like a hot hand went down my throat and it immediately disappeared." My grandmother's story, as well as my mother's experience, created in me a hunger to know God personally and intimately. That kind of spiritual heritage birthed a desire in me not to just know about Him, but to *experience* Him.

I am glad that the experience of feeling Him, being visited by Him, hearing His voice, is not just the domain of the Pentecostals or the Charismatics, but is the privilege of all His children. I am glad that the old spiritual song is true. "I come to the garden alone, while the dew I still on the roses, and He walks with me and He talks to me, and He tells me I am His own." Don't be satisfied with only a head knowledge of God, when the wonder of "knowing" Him experientially is our privilege as a child of His.

One cannot read this book without becoming hungrier for "just a closer walk with Thee" type of experience/relationship. I know that I have a holy jealousy for the intimacy I see for God in Gary Oates' life. I am no longer satisfied to be able to sense the presence of angels when they come near me. I want to see them.

I want to enter into the fulfillment of a word I received over ten years ago, "I want your eyes to be opened to see My resources for you in the heavenlies, just as Elisha prayed for Gehazi's eyes to be opened."

I encourage you to read this book with an open heart and mind. As you do, agree with me in this prayer, *"Open my eyes, Lord...I want to see Jesus...to reach out and touch Him...to tell Him I love Him. Open my eyes, Lord...I want to see. I want to see Your heavenly resources for me. As Elisha prayed for Gehazi, for his eyes to be opened, I pray for every reader of this book to have their eyes opened; just as I pray for my own eyes to be opened. In Jesus' Name. Amen."*

Randy Clark
Global Awakening Ministries
International Conference Speaker
Author, *Lighting Fires*

# Preface

I struggled quite a while with the idea of writing a book. I honestly didn't think a testimony of my experiences was needed, and certainly I wanted no attention drawn to me as a result of my heavenly encounters. That's not what this book is all about.

Yet, I was encouraged by many in the Body of Christ that this message was needed—not just a book about my experiences but also a thorough biblical teaching tool on receiving an impartation to walk in God's supernatural.

If you had told me—prior to June 2002—that my wife, Kathi, and I would be functioning in a ministry of the supernatural, or even writing a book about such experiences, I would have said, "You're crazy!"

But as I have reviewed my life with my friend and co-author, Robert Paul Lamb, a thread of God's prophetic counsel has emerged pointing to the day when this kind of ministry would come forth. For instance, my daily prayer journal from April 24, 1974 records a word from the Lord: "I will see in the spirit world, angels and demons, and the ministry of angels."

On December 1, 1976 while visiting the church Kathi and I were pastoring in Gatlinburg, Tennessee, South African prophet Robert Thom, prayed and prophesied: "Lord, I ask that Thou would give them a supernatural ministry that shall reach the masses..."

In July 1981 during an ordination service, a prophetic minister brought the following word to me: "My son...you are going to be invited to travel and teach, and you will go with a group of ministers to teach the Body of Christ, not only in this country, but in other countries where there is a great need..."

Following a 40-day fast that ended June 20, 1997, I wrote in my journal: "I'm not sure about the following but God seemed to be saying we would be traveling more. I'm an introvert and not good at speaking on the road like others. I don't have a charismatic personality, and I'm certainly not flamboyant or outgoing. But the Lord has said it would be more for ministry in healing and miracles. I would like it to be so but I just don't know."

That last day of the fast, I had been caught in a sudden Florida downpour while out walking. The Lord told me later: "I will come suddenly like the rain. You won't be able to escape it. You will know it is Me."

Even after Kathi and I began having supernatural experiences in 2002 and a worldwide ministry opened to us, I was still struggling with feelings of being inadequate for the overwhelming task. The huge arenas we were ministering in were a far cry from the churches of a few hundred we once pastored.

It was during a prayer time in Brazil with Kathi, Tom Ruotolo and a Brazilian worship leader that I was taken up into God's Presence and He spoke to me. "I have called you and I will do it," He said emphatically.

The voice had such a strong, rich and resonating sound—nothing like I'd ever heard before. It shook me to the core. Every word seemed to penetrate my being.

What a relief! It took all the pressure off...all the striving...all the self-efforts...all the self-imposed performance that most of us experience. All I had to do was learn to trust God and He would do it. I had finally settled the issue with Him. God called me and He was going to do whatever was necessary to complete that calling.

I'm a living example of God using inadequate people for the awesome challenges of ministry. But in my weaknesses, He shows His great strength.

Heidi Baker, who has been greatly used of the Lord among the nations, prophesied over Kathi and me on November 16, 2002: "Within one year from today, you will see more fruit than you have seen in the past twenty years of ministry. Write it down. It will happen."

Actually, Heidi was wrong. It didn't take an entire year. It only took six months!

Praise God! He is so good. I am so grateful—and privileged—to be His servant in this generation, and to witness His mighty works among the nations of the earth.

I am more in love with Jesus now than ever before. I can't get enough of His Presence. The more I have the more I want. My prayer is that this book will ignite that same love in you for Him...that you will go to a higher level of spiritual growth...that the supernatural realm of the Spirit will become the normal Christian life for you.

Gary Oates
Moravian Falls, NC

# Introduction

If you've had an opportunity to hear Gary Oates' testimony of angelic visitations, you might be left with the impression that Gary has lived a charmed existence, rich with deep spiritual experiences and little in the way of challenges, conflicts and problems.

That would be far from an accurate picture. Gary didn't just show up in Brazil one day and angels immediately manifested taking him to new spiritual heights in his relationship with the Lord.

No. Gary has been through a process. A lengthy and invaluable process that began a long time ago and recently culminated in these angelic experiences in Brazil and later in the USA.

Although raised in a Christian home, that embraced strong biblical tenets, Gary Oates was afraid to give his heart to the Lord. Schooled in the Baptist "sword drills"—looking up a verse of Scripture the fastest way possible—he knew the plan of God for an individual's life was nothing to trifle with.

Gary feared his salvation would bring about a "call" to become a missionary in Africa, and he wanted no part of that.    Somehow the "dark continent", as it was known in those days, was a place where Gary did not want to go.

Thus, he held out until age fourteen before accepting the Lord.  The night of his surrender, he even promised Jesus:  "I'm willing to be a missionary to Africa if that's what You want."

It seems from the very beginning Gary Oates had something in his heart about overseas travel and ministering the Gospel.  He just didn't know what that "something" was.

After his marriage to Kathi, he told her about his desire to go to the mission field and reach out to other nations.  She was polite but firm.  Gary could travel anywhere he wanted, but she *wasn't*.

There had been prophetic words throughout their early ministry.  At an ordination once, one of the ministers prophesied over Gary that he would "go to the nations."  Gary thought that was an odd word because of the situation with Kathi.

After pioneering churches in several states, Gary fell into despair and frustration, quitting the ministry for almost four years while working as a stockbroker.  Mad at God, he cared little for prayer or Bible reading and only went to church because of his two young daughters.

Finally, God began to ignite a smoldering wick of a ministerial call in his life. He had faced years of challenge from the devil over whether he'd ever been called or not. Literally, at the end of his rope, Gary had no place else to go but to the Lord. It was the beginning of an incredible breakthrough that would bring him back into ministry.

During another trial—while pastoring in Tallahassee—he began praying that God would open his eyes and show him things from a divine perspective. It was a prayer that would give him vision into an unseen world and change thousands of lives along the way.

And that's the story that essentially unfolds in these pages.

One final note. I have known and admired Gary Oates for more than twenty-five years. I preached for him in the church he and Kathi pioneered in Gatlinburg, Tennessee, and my wife and I attended the church the Oates planted in Roswell, Georgia for several years.

Gary has always been a man of exceptional integrity and grace. I have always known him as a man of God with a true shepherd's heart. But this man, who has been transformed by these heavenly encounters, has become a man of the Spirit   No one could ever be the same again once touched as Gary has.

His example of "wanting more of God" in his own life is an inspiration to all the rest of us who aspire to be used of the Lord in this generation.  My life has been challenged and blessed by simply working together on compiling this book.

*"For our light affliction, which is but for a moment, is working for us a far more exceeding and eternal weight of glory, while we do not look at the things which are seen, but at the things which are not seen.  For the things which are seen are temporary, but the things which are not seen are eternal,"* (2 Corinthians 4:17-18, NKJV).

Robert Paul Lamb
Moravian Falls, NC

# Chapter 1

# THE PRAYER

*"The hunger of a man's soul must be satisfied. It must be satisfied. It is a law of God; that law of God is in the depth of the Spirit. God will answer the heart that cries. God will answer the soul that asks."*

—From a sermon on "Spiritual Hunger" given by noted missionary/preacher John G. Lake in Portland, Oregon on December 11, 1924.

Spring of 2002.

It was an incredibly difficult time for my wife Kathi and I, after pastoring for some thirty years and planting five different churches in various places-- Washington state, Tennessee, Georgia and Florida.

Our church in Tallahassee, Florida's capital city was not large, maybe a little over a hundred people or so. We had started eight years earlier in our living room with a Bible study that had ultimately grown into a spirited congregation with its own rented building.

Then, eight families notified us because of varying reasons of work or family matters that they were moving out of town. One of the families had six children and another had five.

The result was that our once-thriving children's church was gutted. The families were all tithers, so our finances also took a beating.

Then, a situation came up with our worship leader and we had to let him go. Four more families left over that issue. In less than two months, twelve families had left the church. After years of struggle and labor—the kind of effort only a pastor would possibly understand—people were now heading for the exits.

The result was a gnawing frustration inside. I really didn't understand what God was doing. Was He involved in any of this? I began to second-guess myself. Was I out of the will of God in Tallahassee? Was God finished with me in pastoral ministry? Could I ever do anything right again?

The summer time was looming ahead. That was always a slack time in the church for us any way with people on vacation, or simply disappearing to the beach (an hour or so away) whenever the weather was right.

## *The Prayer*

Plans had already been made to participate in a series of meetings sponsored by Randy Clark's Global Awakening ministry in Brazil. Two years earlier, I had gone on my first Global trip to Brazil. That experience was like reliving the book of Acts again and again. I saw all kinds of miracles happening around me, and then, the first person I prayed for—a lame man—walked away healed!

I subsequently prayed for another man in the latter stages of emphysema and also with a hearing problem. God immediately healed the man's lungs and he no longer needed a hearing aid.

Returning to the states I was pumped up and excited about all that the Lord had done. Yet, in time with all the rigors of pastoring, the memory of what God had done in South America faded.

In 2001, I went on another Global trip to Brazil and again, the Lord opened my eyes to the realm of the miraculous. In fact, this trip went to a whole new level in God. But the same thing happened when I returned to the states, everything faded.

When a third Global trip came about for June 2002, I was finally able to talk Kathi into going. She agreed reluctantly but after the money came in for her ticket, she was committed. The trip was only a month or so away and now we had missed six weeks of paychecks. Kathi felt guilty about going and wanted to use her trip money for paychecks.

Between the struggle with finances and all the church departures in April and May, I didn't even feel like going myself. How could I be of any value feeling as low as I did? What help could I be?

"Lord," I began to pray, "I have more need of ministry myself than I feel I can possibly give out to others. How will I be of any use on this trip?"

For weeks, it seemed as if I struggled over this trip. Should I go or not? What difference could I make in others' lives? How could I help anybody when my need was so great? Then, unexplainably a resolution began to grow in me. I was desperate— great need or not—I had to have a touch from God myself.

Somewhere along the way, my prayer changed. It went from telling God how I felt to making a request. "Lord, I pray that You will open my eyes on this trip so that I can see what You're doing. I want to see things from Your perspective."

Looking back, I know God was directing these prayers. "Lord, I want to see beyond the natural...I want to see angels...I want to see into the realm of the Spirit," I prayed.

It was a little prayer of desperation prayed by a man who was helpless without God. Yet, it was destined to radically change my life. I had hit rock bottom and something had to change. I had never felt such desperation for God.

## *The Prayer*

Life would never be the same again. It would not be the same for me, or Kathi, or those whose lives we would be able to touch. God would soon be walking into our lives with great power. Everything about us would be different—forever.

## Chapter 2

# "UP IS BETTER..."

*"Believers, look up--take courage. The angels are nearer than you think."*

—Billy Graham from the book, *Angels: God's Secret Agents*

**D**uring our travels in Brazil on that trip, we were transported mostly by bus from one city to the next. It was during one of those days as we traveled down a bustling Brazilian highway from Petropolis to Volta Redonda that I recognized Randy Clark was conducting an interview with a worship leader with Casa de Davi, traveling with us.

He has experienced angelic visitations on a regular basis, and Randy was asking all kinds of questions about these visitations. I was glued to their words.

Sitting across the aisle from the worship

leader, I tapped him on the shoulder when his conversation with Randy ended. "That's what I want," I volunteered pointing to my eyes.

The worship leader doesn't speak English but he seemed to grasp what I was saying. He reached over and placed his left hand on my right hand. When he did, my hand started having an unusual tingling sensation.

He left his hand there for the longest time, never really saying a word. I wasn't sure what was happening although I felt an impartation taking place I didn't fully understand.

Our bus arrived at its destination, and I stood up to leave. The worship leader was standing there, so I gave him a hug. When I did, the Spirit of God came over me and my knees began to buckle. Tears began flowing down my cheeks.

As we were leaving the bus that day for a lunch stop, I found myself walking along with Mike Shea, who heads up the prophetic ministry/worship team of Casa de Davi. An American who has lived more than twenty years in Brazil as a missionary, Mike is both a gifted musician and minister of the Gospel.

"Mike, have you had experiences like what the worship leader has experienced?" I asked as we strolled toward the restaurant.

"To a little degree," he smiled, "but not like anything he has experienced."

"Tell me about it," I pursued. "How can this be activated? What can I do?"

"Romans 6:13," he answered.

"Romans 6:13?"

"Yeah."

"What does that say?" I asked.

"We are not to submit the members of our body as instruments of sin and unrighteousness but to present the members of our bodies as instruments of holiness," he answered.

I was puzzled. I thought, "What does that have to do with it?"

Seeing my expression, Mike explained: "When we're talking about the members of our bodies, let's focus on the five senses—our eyes and our spiritual vision of seeing these things. We're talking about eyes, our ears, our mouth, our nose and our hands. It's a matter of giving them over to the Lord."

Understanding began to come to me. I

realized our five senses are the entry points and the access points of all the worldly and demonic influences we come up against every day.

These are also the very places for the Holy Spirit and the power of God to be released in us. The problem is we're yielding our five senses in the wrong areas and not to the Lord.

That very afternoon—before the meeting where I had my first angelic visitation—I took out my Bible and read Romans 6:13. *"And do not go on presenting the members of your body to sin as instruments of unrighteousness; but present yourselves to God as those alive from the dead, and your members as instruments of righteousness to God."*

Then, I slowly and verbally committed my five senses to the Lord.

"I give You my eyes that I might see from Your perspective...

"Lord, I give You my ears that I can hear Your voice more clearly...

"Lord, I give You my mouth that I might speak Your words...

"God, I give You my nose that I might smell Your sweet fragrance...

"God, I give You my hands that they might be used in serving You...

"I give You my whole person—spirit, soul and body. God, I give You my whole being. I withhold nothing from You. Everything I have is Yours. Everything I am is Yours. I give it all to You. I lay my life on the altar before You. I yield myself totally and completely to You...

"Lord, I give You my whole person."

Lying there on the bed, I sensed a strong Presence of the Lord in the room. Somehow I felt I had connected with God's heart.

Later that night, we gathered for the church service in a huge tent that seated some 3,000. The worship at the service was simply awesome. It was what I'd call "off the charts". The place was electric with the Presence of the Lord. It was while I was worshipping with my hands raised and praising God that He began to speak to me.

"Take your shoes off," He instructed. "You're standing on holy ground."

My first reaction was negative. It was a dusty, dirty concrete floor. I didn't really want to take my shoes off. I continued worshipping.

A few minutes later, the Lord spoke again. "Take your shoes off."

"Wait a minute," I thought to myself. "This is the Lord. I'd better do this."

Immediately I reached down and took off my

41

shoes. It was a small act of obedience—obedience in something that seemed insignificant—that set the stage for the miraculous to follow. God requires obedience in the small things before He will entrust greater things to us. I honestly believe that what followed would have not happened if I hadn't obeyed the Lord in taking off my shoes.

As I looked up at the worship team, the Lord opened my eyes and I saw two Brazilian dancers with three angels dancing around them.

"What is that?" I thought.

Right behind them were two more dancers and three angels around them. On the other side, there were individual dancers and each one of them had a big angel arched over them. The angel followed the dancers' every move.

"Lord, what is going on?" I pondered. "Am I losing my mind?"

Then, it suddenly occurred to me. "This is what I've been asking God for but I evidently wasn't expecting it. I surely didn't know what it was going to be like."

It seemed as if I could see right through the angels. They appeared in a white transparent color. I could see their form and what they were doing. There was great brightness to their appearance and I noted they each had wings.

As a natural response, I looked up above the platform and it was just full of angels and they were all worshipping the Lord. Light danced and swirled about them. There must have been a hundred of these worshipping angels. They were singing, playing instruments, and dancing. The worship was reaching a level of intensity that I hadn't experienced before and the Presence of God began to fill the auditorium.

Standing there with my hands raised worshipping the Lord, I suddenly began to feel myself somehow expanding—getting both bigger and taller. I felt 15 feet tall. I found myself looking down at everybody worshipping the Lord.

"Wow, this is really cool," I thought.

Then, I started going upwards, leaving the floor and also my physical body behind. I was not aware of my physical body or any physical limitations. It was as if my physical body was non-existent. I went higher and higher into the peak of the tent. I was floating there in the top of the tent looking down over the worshipers.

Fear jumped on my insides. "God, this is getting too much," I muttered. Somehow I was resisting what God wanted to do and immediately I started to descend. Realizing what had just happened, I cried out, "No, Lord, forgive me, forgive me...up is better...up is better!"

Instantly, I reversed direction and accelerated at a great speed going straight up, right through the top of the tent (just like Superman) and into the heavenlies. The fabric of the tent was no obstacle as I passed straight through it. I found myself looking down over part of the city and I could see the top of the tent glowing with the Presence of God.

I was not living under the bondage of a physical body. It seemed as if I was living in a limitless state—not bound by time or space. It was an incredible feeling as though nothing were impossible. Really, no words can adequately describe what that truly felt like.

Somehow I had zoom vision and could see right through the tent. There was a divine radiance at the top of the tent. A big hole opened in the tent's roof and I saw people worshipping the Lord and the glory of God being poured out in that place.

Then, fear nailed me again. "Man, I am really out of control," I thought.

I have always been one of those guys who likes to have everything under control. I like to have all my ducks in a row, and I don't like to get out of my box. Only now, I was way, way, way out of my box—out of my comfort zone.

Again, I was resisting what God was doing, and I started back down. I realized He would only take me as far as I was willing to allow Him, but I was the bottleneck. I put the brakes on. I was the one who would determine how far I went with Him. Because of insecurities or a fear of the supernatural,

## "Up Is Better..."

I had somehow drawn a line in the sand with God.

I came all the way down just inside the tent. My head was right in the top of the canvas. A sense of regret came over me. I honestly believe I could have gone all the way into God's throne room if I hadn't resisted. It was much like the experience of the prophet Ezekiel in only going part way to God's throne, *"...and the Spirit lifted me up between earth and heaven and brought me in the visions of God..."* (Ezekiel 8:3). He didn't go all the way...and neither did I.

Then, I raised my arms as an act of surrender. They seemed to be a mile long as I stretched them through the tent into the sky. I began to cry out to the Lord. "God, I want more of You," I cried. "I want more of You."

As I was looking up, I saw Jesus at a distance coming down towards me. He was full-bodied and wearing a robe. His hands were extended out as my hands were turned up. He took my hands and held them tightly as if to say: "I'm not going to let you go."

There was such a powerful Presence about Him. I didn't find myself turning away from His face. I was glued to it. Yet, His features seemed to be hidden in the brightness of His glory.

When He took my left hand, it was a strong grip. My left hand began to burn in a little spot that got bigger and bigger until the whole palm of my hand was on fire. I didn't know if I could take it any more with the power and Presence of God working within me.  At that moment, He released me back into my body.

Having been in the Presence of the Lord, I virtually exploded when I came back into my natural physical body.  It seemed my body could not contain my spirit after such a heavenly experience.  The shock of coming back into my body catapulted me backwards as if I had done a backward swan dive.  I hit three rows of chairs and then the concrete floor.  Nobody caught me.  It was as if I had landed on a bed of feathers.  I didn't feel a thing.

For about an hour, I lay on the floor.  I couldn't move, not even a muscle.  I had no understanding of what had just happened to me.  I felt so little and insignificant in the presence of such a holy God.  Again, I found myself crying out to God, "I want more of You, Lord.... I just want more of You.... I want more of You."

Finally, I was able to rouse myself, pull myself into a chair and put my shoes back on.  I could hardly speak.  If I had, it probably wouldn't have made sense to anyone.  I was still trying to grasp what had happened.  I felt physically drained and emotionally depleted.

The prophet Isaiah described himself as *"undone and ruined"* after he had seen the Lord (Isaiah 6:5).  That comes very close to what I had experienced.

Kathi was bewildered at what had happened

to me. We went back into a room for refreshments after the service but I could hardly talk. People were asking me questions—nonstop. I was crying, virtually incoherent in speech and still shaken from my experience. I didn't know if I could find the words to explain what had happened.

The next morning I was dragging around as if I had been in a drunken stupor the night before. Somebody would have to take my hand and direct me to where we were going.

One of the women on the team came up, looked me in the face and asked: "Gary, are you okay? Are you okay physically?'

"No, physically, I'm shot," I answered. "I'm completely wasted."

"Are you okay spiritually?" she asked.

"Well," I responded with a little twinkle in my eye, "spiritually, I'm through the roof!"

## Chapter 3

# "GOD, I WANT MORE OF YOU..."

*"The secret of spiritual success is a hunger that persists...It is an awful condition to be satisfied with one's spiritual attainments...God was and is looking for hungry, thirsty people."*

—Smith Wigglesworth, (1859-1947), the famed Apostle of Faith

The next night before the meeting began, I took a seat on the front row. Shortly afterwards, the worship leader walked up and sat down one seat over. He smiled at me and then placed his hand on my left shoulder.

When he did the power of God surged through me and I fell like a dead man on the chair between us, trapping my arm between my chest and the chair. Several guys saw my predicament, moved the chair out of the way and laid me down on the floor.

Again, I couldn't move. It seemed as if my body weighed ten tons. I felt like I was being pressed against the floor. All the while I was crying out, "God, I want more of You.... I want more of You.... I want more of You".

By this time, the worship team was up ministering, and I could see them on the platform. All of a sudden, the picture changed before me and I didn't see the team any more. Instead, I saw a golden path coming down the aisle and going up some golden steps onto a gold platform. Above that, there were more steps to a higher gold platform.

On top of the last platform, I saw a throne and Jesus standing on the right hand side of the throne with a scepter in his hand. The throne was a large ornate chair but I saw nobody sitting in the chair. But neither the scepter nor the throne drew my attention.

The Lord was my focus, and I could see his whole torso. He didn't appear in the robe I had seen Him wearing before but it appeared to be some kind of pants. A divine radiance or a divine light was emanating from His head to His waist. It is nearly impossible to describe how bright and how penetrating the light was. It was so bright it could pin you to the wall with its clarity.

The brilliance of the Lord's appearance agreed completely with the words of Mark 9:3, *"And His garments became radiant and exceedingly white, as no launderer on earth can whiten them.*

Standing no more than fifty feet away from the Lord in the midst of His light, I felt like I was going to die. I honestly felt this was the end. There was no way I could survive this. In fact, I thought maybe I had died and gone to heaven. It was that real.

At that moment, I came back to myself writhing in agony on the floor. Kathi got scared looking at the terror in my face. I was twisting in anguish with my arms around my midsection. My mouth was open trying to scream but no sound was coming out. I was in torment. Terror flooded my being. "Do something," she insisted to some men standing nearby, "help him."

"He's okay," said one of the guys reassuringly. "Turn around. Don't even look at him."

Kathi and the people standing near her were concerned about me. They could have hardly known the reason for my terror and agony. I had become acutely aware of my sinfulness in the Presence of a Holy God.

I saw the glory of God like I had never seen it before, and I found myself crying out, "God, forgive me.... forgive me. Lord, I just want more of You.... more of You."

It seemed to take me forever to even get up from the floor. I lost all sense of time. I was later told I had been on the floor for two hours. Since I couldn't walk, two of the team members, Chuck Snekvik and Marcus Morris, helped me up and walked me outside for some fresh air. They were literally holding me up by the elbows. Later they brought me back inside where Kathi and I took an empty seat on the back row.

Randy Clark was preaching about a time his mother was taken up before the Lord. As he shared, the Presence of the Lord flowed over me like bolts of electricity going through my body. I was shaking and trembling so much I could hardly sit in the chair.

I felt I was about to explode on the inside as he preached. I began to relive all these experiences that had just occurred with being taken into God's Presence.

"Are you gonna be okay?" Kathi asked. "Are you all right?".

"Yeah," I mumbled.

"Well, what happened?" she quizzed. "What happened to you?"

"I can't tell you," I muttered. I was so shaken by what had just happened it seemed to soon to even talk about it. I needed to "process" it before I told anybody—even my wife.

I continued vibrating under the Presence of the Lord. As I looked up, I saw a big angel standing beside Randy as he preached. The angel would lean down and whisper into Randy's ear, and then he would start preaching under a heavy anointing. Unquestionably, everything Randy was preaching was coming straight from the mouth of God.

Every word carried such weight and was penetrating my whole being. I was again shaking and trembling intensely. It was as if I was hearing the voice of God speak through Randy in a way I had not heard His voice before.

Kathi began asking again about what had happened. I could just barely speak but I finally said, "I'll tell you but promise me you won't tell a soul." She agreed and I told her as best I could what had occurred.

Finally, Randy sent word that he wanted me to come up on the platform and assist him during the ministry time. I didn't know if I could walk that far I felt so weak and wasted.

"If You want me to do this, You'll have to give me the strength to go down there," I told the Lord. "I don't have it otherwise." Yet as the meeting progressed, I slowly became strengthened.

The same two guys, Chuck and Marcus, volunteered to get me down to the platform. I had prayed for a young man on the way to the front and the Presence of the Lord overwhelmed me again. Even though the building was packed and running over with people, the fellows were finally able to get me into a chair at the front.

"Now, Gary Oates is going to come up and tell us what has happened to him," Randy was telling the audience.

By this time, I could barely stay in the chair where I sat with my arms bent over and my hands dragging the floor. I could hardly speak. Obviously, I was in no condition to do what Randy had just announced.

"Pick him up in the chair and bring him up here," Randy instructed the two guys helping me.

I was still trembling and vibrating as they picked me up and carried me onto the platform. I felt utterly helpless in that condition.

Randy walked over trying to get me to explain what had happened, but I couldn't speak. Finally, he called Kathi forward. "I want Gary's wife to come up and tell us what's happened to him," he announced.

Kathi took the microphone and then suddenly remembered she'd promised not to say anything. She came over and asked if it was okay to tell. Since I was shaking so vigorously with my head bobbing up and down, she took that as a "yes".

As she began to tell what had happened to me, the Spirit of God fell in that place. People were crying out; others were falling on their face in repentance. Tears were flowing. Some were getting healed. God was doing a spontaneous, yet miraculous work in that church.

Finally, Randy said "I want all the pastors to come up because I want Gary Oates to lay hands on them and pray over them."

"How am I gonna do that?" I wondered.

I couldn't get my hands off the floor. I had no strength in my hands and I couldn't stop shaking. I was bent over with my chest on my knees. I couldn't even straighten up. In truth, I couldn't do anything at that moment.

Randy instructed my two helpers, Chuck and Marcus, to lift my hands and lay them on each pastor's head. The first pastor walked up to be prayed for. Seeing me bent over in the chair, he got down on the floor and crawled to a place where my shaking hands could be placed on his head. As soon as my hands touched the pastor's head, he went out in the Spirit.

The ushers dragged him off and brought another pastor forward. Again, the same thing happened. He crawled underneath my hands and went out. The same happened to every pastor in that line.

I felt absolutely stupid. Foolish. Inside I was saying to the Lord, "What's this all about? I'm an introvert...a reserved guy and here I'm up here just making a fool out of myself."

"I use the foolish things to confound the wise," the Lord reminded me.

"I'm willing to be a fool for You if that's what You want," I replied. "You can use me anyway that You want. I don't understand this stuff but I'm just yielding to You. I want You to do whatever You need to do." I knew I was totally out of control.

After each pastor had been touched, the two team members went off to pray for others and I ultimately just fell out of the chair onto the floor. I was stretched out on the floor for some time when I overheard Kathi's voice praying for people.

"Gary, pray for this baby," she finally said to me. "Put your hand on this baby."

"I can't," I mumbled.

"Yes, you can," she suggested, "just reach back here."

"I can't.... I can't move it," I slurred.

Taking matters into her hands, she grabbed my left hand, placed it on the baby's head and prayed. It wasn't that I didn't want to pray. I was having a hard time thinking, much less praying.

My right hand was extended outwards. I couldn't move my hand but I felt people touching it, and then I felt something wet and oily in my hand. With all the strength I could muster, I was able to move my head to a place where I could see my right hand.

I was shocked at what I saw!  A man poured a bottle of anointing oil on my right hand, got on his hands and knees, did a headstand, smacked his head down into my hand and rubbed it around. When he finished, another man came and did the same thing.  A girl followed him, and there seemed to be a line of people after her.

In hindsight I realized it was not about me; it was about the Lord.  I had never seen such hunger in the hearts of people that they would do such foolish things themselves.   Yet, I was merely a contact point, a conduit of what God was doing.

Finally, I was able to get myself into a sitting position on the floor.  I grabbed onto a chair and ultimately seated myself again.  People saw me sitting up and came forward for prayer.  By then, I could raise my hands up enough that I could actually lay hands on them and pray for them.

Then, the Lord nudged me to stand up and minister to the people.  I resisted temporarily but a divine energy came into me and I stood upright.  I began praying for people and a long line formed. Almost everybody I prayed for indicated they were healed.  They manifested the Presence of God so strongly with many of them falling down. All kinds of healings were taking place without any effort on my part.  I knew it was truly a ministry of the Holy Spirit.

# Chapter 4

# ANGELS IN RIO & ATLANTA

*"The invisible realm is superior to the natural. The reality of that invisible dominates the natural world we live in...both positively and negatively..."*

—Pastor Bill Johnson from the book, *When Heaven Invades Earth*

**T**he next night we traveled to a large church in Rio de Janeiro, Brazil's second largest city and its former capital city. The place was overflowing with people, and as a result, the ministry team had to take seats on the huge platform.

While we were worshipping the Lord, the worship leader motioned to the drummer, Lucio de Paula, and he began something like an impassioned drum solo. The drums kept building and building in intensity. Goose bumps broke out on my body.

Standing there in the midst of this drumming, the Lord spoke to me "warfare". Then, He said: "Open your eyes."

Right where the ceiling and the wall come together I saw a host of angels flooding into the room. It was the first time I saw them in an appearance other than a milk-like transparency. Their appearance was so vivid and distinct. It was almost like seeing another person—but not quite.

These were war angels wearing pewter-looking armor and carrying two-edged swords in their hands that were just glistening. The angels were all different sizes—some big, others smaller. Actually they were not as large as I would have thought war angels would have been.

Their gleaming swords were all proportionate to the size of the angels. Bigger angels had larger swords, and smaller angels smaller swords. They were swinging those swords as they moved through the room, and it seemed the size of the angel had nothing to do with the power that particular angel manifested.

Although the angels were moving so fast you could hardly see them, the objects of their furor were black blobs all around the room. The angels would hit those blobs with their swords and they'd literally disappear. It was just like dive bombers going through that place cleaning it out.

"This is too much," I pondered. "I *know* I

must be losing my mind."

Afterwards, I questioned the worship leader about what happened during the drum solo. "It was warfare," he explained. "There was a group of war angels that came in and cleaned the room out of all the demons." He had seen exactly the same thing. Thank God, I wasn't losing my mind after all.

The next night in the same church, the Lord nudged me "to turn around and look down the middle aisle". As I looked, a group of worshipping angels, totally different in appearance than the other angels, came joyously dancing down the aisle as if they were ushering the Presence of the Lord into the service. These worshipping angels came part way down the aisle, swooped around meeting together in the back, then again proceeded into the church.

The angels then marched behind two doors on the church's stage. I didn't understand immediately what the angels were doing until later when the church had a drama skit. Behind the two large doors was the throne of God and the four living creatures. For some reason, these worshipping angels were congregating there.

A day later in another church in Rio, Randy Clark asked me to pray for a man in his seventies who was suffering from brain cancer. "Get some of the team members," Randy said, "and go back with the pastor and pray for this man."

As we gathered in a circle, the Brazilian pastor said to me, "this man and his wife do not know the

Lord. He's had brain surgery and the doctors are saying he doesn't have long to live." With that, he gave me a bottle of anointing oil.

In the past my approach had always been "a little dab will do ya." But the Lord seemed to show me to cup my right hand and fill it with oil. I took my hand full of oil and placed it on the man's head. Oil splattered and ran everywhere--down his forehead, eyes, and nose, off his ears and onto his shirt.

"I may be blowing this big time," I thought to myself. "This guy doesn't know the Lord and here I am slapping oil on him. He may be trying to figure all this out." To my surprise, my approach didn't seem to bother him.

One of the team members got paper napkins and wiped the man off and then I began to pray. As I did I saw two white, translucent wings with a silver sheen come out of nowhere and wrap around this man. This angel must have been big because the wings were especially large even though they didn't cover the man completely.

It was a touching scene as the angel put his wings around the man. I could see this man's countenance soften even though he didn't know what was happening. Yet, he was obviously sensing God's comfort and peace that was coming over him.

I was standing a little to the left of the man as I was praying for him. Then, I suddenly noticed a second, smaller angel to the right of the other angel, and this second angel was blowing fire like a blowtorch into the left side of the man's forehead.

When I saw the fire, I did a double take. "What in the world?" I wondered. I never expected to see anything like that, and I looked again just to be sure. "Oh, my goodness," I muttered.

"Are you sensing anything?" I asked the man. "Are you feeling anything?"

"Yeah, my head feels like it's on fire...it's burning up," he said. "I'm healed...I know I'm healed."

"Well, that's great," I replied, "but I want you to get a confirmation. Go back to your doctor and have him verify the healing."

"No, I'm healed," the man said.

"Well, I think you are too," I said firmly. "But, please...go get it confirmed." He finally agreed.

One of the team members spoke up. "Neither this guy nor his wife know the Lord," she reminded me. "They're not saved."

I then remembered what the church's pastor had said. With the help of my interpreter, we gave the man a brief plan of salvation and asked, "Would you like to invite Jesus Christ into your heart right now?"

He looked at me and replied, "No."

63

"I beg your pardon?" I quizzed in astonishment.

"No!"

"No?" I asked again.

He looked at me and said "no."

"You mean after all that just happened with your healing," I began. "Are you serious about telling the Lord 'no'. Why?"

"If I get saved in this church, I'll have to attend here," he said simply.

"It's not about religion," I explained. "It's about a relationship. If you get saved here, you can go to any church you want to. It's important that you find a good church that believes the Bible and that includes a belief in healing and miracles."

The man began to smile. "Okay, then, I'll get saved," he enthused. It was a precious moment that pulled at the strings of our hearts as the couple held hands and gave their lives to the Lord. Most of the team members had tears in their eyes as we finished praying.

\*　　\*　　\*　　\*　　\*

One afternoon after I had been caught up before the Lord, we had a meeting of the ministry team for prayer. Although Kathi had reluctantly gone on the trip, she had told me she wasn't being left out of what God was doing—especially after what had happened to me! That afternoon she was determined to be prayed over.

We had enjoyed a meal in the church's cafeteria. Then, spontaneously the worship leader picked up his guitar. Instead of strumming it, however, he began to pound out a rhythm on the guitar. Then, Lucio (the drummer) grabbed some drink coolers and began to drum them. People began to leap and dance before the Lord. It seemed the angels were joining together with us in this chorus of percussion.

Mike Shea began to blow the shofar over people. I was already down on the floor when he blew the shofar at my side sending a reverberation into my spirit. A few minutes later he blew the shofar over Kathi. She went "out", was totally drunk in the Spirit and could not move for quite a long time.

By the time the wave of percussion had subsided, Kathi saw the worship leader across the room and crawled on her hands and knees to reach him for prayer. Unable to stand, she slid down his knees—three times! After that prayer, she had to be carried to the bus for our trip back to the hotel. She could not speak intelligibly for several hours.

She told me later that when she was on the floor under the Holy Spirit's power she had a vision of standing before God's throne in heaven. In the vision the Lord asked her to empty her pockets of what she thought were shiny prized possessions.

But the possessions were literally junk—defense mechanisms, pride, judgment. She found herself lying at the Lord's feet where a great cleansing was taking place.

Then the Lord handed her a gold coin. "Take this and eat it," He said. "What is it, Lord?" she asked. "It's the gold of the kingdom," He answered. In obedience she did.

Somehow—whether from Mike's blowing of the shofar, or the worship leader's prayer over her, or her throne room vision—Kathi was immediately launched into a new realm of powerfully sharpened prophetic utterances and seeing angels as well!

Kathi's new unction began the very next night in a Baptist Church in Rio de Janeiro. It was an overflow crowd of perhaps 700 people jammed into a building that would normally seat over 500, with at least a thousand more in the parking lot watching the service on a large video screen.

As we stood on the platform during an altar call, God opened Kathi's eyes—for the first time—to see angels. She turned to me and said, "There's an angel standing behind that woman." She pointed to a woman in the balcony saying, "She's gonna be healed."

A woman standing beside me spoke up. "That lady is a close friend and she's the head intercessor in this church," she explained. She motioned for the woman to come downstairs although Kathi felt she could be healed where she stood.

Kathi made her way down through the crowd and met the woman backstage. The anointing was so strong when she prayed for the woman she was "out" instantly and slid down the wall to the floor. Kathi returned to the auditorium and began praying for every person who had an angel standing behind him or her. The results were amazing: healings for curvature of the spine, female problems, eyesight, and hearing.

It was uncanny. Every time Kathi saw an angel behind someone, she prayed and the healings manifested.

In a meeting in South Florida, a woman had been touched in the services but wanted extra prayer for her back. Immediately, Kathi saw the angel standing behind the woman. She acknowledged the angel's presence and then began praying for the woman.

The woman in her fifties suddenly began twisting around, and then it seemed she began a whipping motion, accompanied by gyrations and backbends—things in the natural that probably would have hurt anyone's back. The woman's pain totally left her.

Kathi and I were not only united in marriage as one, but we had now experienced parallel encounters with the angelic.

Randy Clark commented a number of times how unusual it was for both husband and wife to have such parallel experiences.  But we did!

*     *     *     *     *

Two months later Kathi and I were attending a conference sponsored by Nehemiah Ministries in Atlanta.  The conference, arranged by Michael Ellis, was their first International School of Ministry where students from different parts of the world come for an intensive two-month training program.

Randy Clark, Heidi Baker, a missionary to Mozambique, and Henry Madava, Pastor of the second largest church in the Ukraine, were among the speakers.  During Randy's time of ministry, he called me to the platform where I shared a portion of my testimony.

The next day Henry Madava was preaching. During the ministry time, I was standing there when suddenly my guardian angel surrounded me with his arms and was holding me very tight.  In fact, he was literally squeezing me.

This particular angel has become my friend, and I know, when he shows up, everything is under control.  The angel had never done this before, and I began thinking, "What is he doing?  Why is he doing this?"

When my eyes were first opened to see the angels in Brazil, the worship leader had commented several times that he had seen my guardian angel.

68

According to the worship leader, this angel was tall—maybe nine or ten feet in height—and he had seen him standing behind me or beside me on several occasions.

Pondering over the possibility of having a guardian angel, I began closely examining the Scriptures. Then, I came across Matthew 18:10, *"...for I tell you that in heaven their angels always are in the presence of and look upon the face of My Father Who is in heaven,"* (Amplified).

The word "their" suggests a personal connection between an individual and an angel. Some theological books have suggested "their angels" are likely guardian angels of the highest rank because they "always see the face of My Father."

I found in my study that Matthew 18:10 certainly agrees with the words of Psalm 91:11. *"For He will give His angels [especial] charge over you to accompany and defend and preserve you in all your ways [of obedience and service],"* (Amplified).

Thus, I began to accept the belief God had provided a guardian angel for my benefit and assistance. While in Brazil, I couldn't recall seeing this angel, but he appeared at our first church service when we returned to Tallahassee. I had been seated on the front row during the worship service and I suddenly saw this angel on the platform. Immediately, I knew this was *my* guardian angel.

I saw this angel in a white transparent form with his wings extended outward. It was a form I would see him in at times when I was due to

69

minister. He would be standing with the worship team or beside the podium. I began to trust the divine flow of God in my life when I saw that angel appear.

But that day in Atlanta, something was different about the angel's actions. I just wasn't sure what.

"If the Lord is touching you right now, please come down front," Pastor Madava instructed, and I made a beeline down to the front. I was just standing and waiting on the Lord when my angel came over and held me again seemingly in a lock grip—only this time, he seemed to be squeezing me more.

"What's he doing?" I pondered again. "Why is he doing it?"

All of a sudden, we took off skyward. The only thing I can compare it to is the space shuttle and the booster rockets. I was the space shuttle and he was the booster rocket, and we just blasted off.

In a moment's time, he took me right into the Presence of God. I saw these dark gray clouds—like storm clouds—swirling around. There were bright lights flashing like strobe lights and lightning, and everything in the distance seemed to light up.

In a blur the angel and I passed by creatures that were bowing down and worshipping God. I momentarily had the thought that must be the four living creatures.

As I looked through the clouds, I was awed by what I saw. Eyes of fire—deep red, penetrating eyes—were drawing closer to me. They were eyes that nothing could possibly hide from--not in heaven or earth. I was overcome with a respectful fear of the living God.

Then, my attention was drawn above the eyes, and I saw thick, wavy, flowing white hair appearing through the clouds. I saw no form of a body and could make no distinction of a face as well.

The next thing I knew, my angel picked me up and put me in the Lord's lap in almost a fetal position. The moment was overwhelming. I felt a deep peace and a sense of comfort that I can hardly describe. It seemed like the angel wanted to show me around or tell me more but it never happened.

Then, boom!

I came back into my body standing at the altar with my hands raised—the very same position I had been in before my experience with the angel. It was at that very moment Pastor Madava laid hands on me as I came back into my body.

I went down and was "out" for the longest time. Soaking in the Lord's Presence, I continually cried out, "I want more of You.... I want more of You.... I want more of You."

At times, I struggled over the awesome experiences of what happened to me in Rio and

Atlanta.  For a long time, it was difficult to talk about such things.  I am probably one of the least likely people to be having these kind of supernatural experiences.

Because of my Baptist background, I wanted a biblical confirmation of all that I had experienced.  It was during a devotional time that the Lord began to further open the Scriptures to me.  He alone knew it was the perfect way to settle my heart about this new dimension of His Spirit working so mightily in our lives.  He first showed me Psalm 97:1-5 (*author's emphasis*),

> *The Lord reigns; Let the earth rejoice; Let the many islands be glad.*
> ***Clouds and thick darkness surround Him;*** *Righteousness and justice are the foundation of His throne.*
> *Fire goes before Him, And burns up His adversaries round about.*
> *His **lightnings** lit up the world; The earth saw and trembled.*
> *The mountains melted like wax at the presence of the Lord, At the presence of the Lord of the whole earth.*

I had not understood the clouds and darkness around the Lord.  It didn't look like what I thought it would.  But it certainly agreed with the words of the Scriptures, including Psalm 18:11-12,

> *He made darkness His hiding place, His canopy around Him, darkness of waters, thick clouds of the skies.*

_From the brightness before Him passed His thick clouds...and coals of fire._

As I studied further, I found Revelation 1:14 that confirmed the Lord's appearance. _"His head and hair were white like white wool, like snow; and His eyes were like a flame of fire."_

I saw exactly what the apostle John saw!

In Revelation 4:1-8 (_author's emphasis_), I came across an entire passage that described the activities around the throne of God:

_After these things I looked, and behold, a door standing open in heaven, and the first voice which I had heard, like the sound of a trumpet speaking with me, said, "Come up here, and I will show you what must take place after these things."_
_Immediately I was in the Spirit; and behold, a throne was standing in heaven, and One sitting on the throne._
_And He who was sitting was like a jasper stone and a sardius in appearance; and there was a rainbow around the throne, like an emerald in appearance._
_Around the throne were twenty-four thrones; and upon the thrones I saw twenty-four elders sitting, clothed in white garments, and golden crowns on_

*their heads.*

**Out from the throne came flashes of lightning and sounds and peals of thunder.** *And there were seven lamps of fire burning before the throne, which are the seven Spirits of God;*

*And before the throne there was something like a sea of glass, like crystal; and in the center and around the throne, four living creatures full of eyes in front and behind.*

*The first creature was like a lion, and the second creature like a calf, and the third creature had a face like that of a man, and the fourth creature was like a flying eagle.*

*And the four living creatures, each one of them having six wings, are full of eyes around and within; and day and night they do not cease to say,*

*"Holy, holy, holy is the Lord God, The Almighty, Who was and Who is and Who is to come."*

\*       \*       \*       \*       \*

The next day at that same conference in Atlanta, Pastor Henry Madava spoke about the fire of God. He quoted Psalm 104:4, *"Who makes winds His messengers, flames of fire His ministers,"* (Amplified). He connected this verse to the Body of Christ as the servants of the Lord who are to be "full of the fire of God."

I saw an angel about twice Pastor Madava's

height (perhaps twelve feet tall) standing behind him. The angel was wearing a robe-like garment and had his arms stretched out. He was large and powerful-looking, and a brilliant glow came from his presence. Everywhere Pastor Madava walked, the angel accompanied him.

As the altar time came, Pastor Madava began to invite the power of God to fall in the auditorium. "Let Your F-I-R-E fall in this place," he prayed passionately. "Let every person in this room be filled with the fire of God."

I saw a row of angels above the platform and they were dispersing a wall of fire over the sanctuary. It was like a huge sheet or blanket of fire coming out and developing into individual flames of gold and orange fire. Those flames turned into balls of fire that suddenly began falling on each person in the room.

"Pay attention to what's happening," the Lord spoke to me.

The balls of fire were hitting people who were open and hungry. They received instantly. Others were sitting there casually observing what was happening. The balls of fire were bouncing above their heads but didn't hit them for a while. Then, I noticed their countenance began to change. As they yielded to the Holy Spirit, instantly the balls of fire would hit them.

But there were others where the balls of fire hovered over for a period of time. Eventually though, the balls of fire floated away and disappeared. These

OPEN MY EYES, LORD

people never received.

"What's this all about?" I wondered.

The Lord began to show me there were three groups of people. Those who received instantly were yielded to God. The second group received slowly as they eventually surrendered to what God was doing, and then they were struck by the balls of fire.

But the last group did not receive at all. I asked the Lord, why didn't they receive? His response was because of areas of pride, control issues and addictions in their lives that were not yielded to Him. These obstacles were preventing them from receiving this great blessing from God. These people never received at all—what was available to everyone!

## Chapter 5

# THE MINISTRY OF ANGELS

*"Scripture makes it clear that God wants us to be aware of the existence of angels and of the nature of their activity. We should not therefore assume that its teaching about angels has nothing whatsoever to do with our lives today. Rather, there are several ways in which our Christian lives will be enriched by an awareness of the existence and ministry of angels in the world today."*

—Wayne Grudem from *Systematic Theology*

The Bible asks a rather remarkable question in Hebrews 1:14 about angels. *"Are they not all ministering spirits, sent out to render service for the sake of those who will inherit salvation?"*

The angels are here to assist the heirs of salvation—the believers—in their God-called tasks upon this earth.  In studying the Scripture, one can conclude they are created spirit beings that can become visible when necessary.

Martin Luther, the great German reformer, has been quoted as saying; "An angel is a spiritual creature without a body created by God for the service of Christendom and the church."

In referring to Hebrews 1:14, the *Spirit Filled Life Bible* says:  "They 'minister' (Greek *diakonia*), referring to their 'serviceable labor, assistance.' They are ministering spirits, or heavenly assistants, who are continually active today..."

### Angelic Intervention

Acts 12:6-17 is wonderful example of an angel being sent from the Lord to rescue Peter from imprisonment and possible execution.  It was during Passover that Peter was jailed, shortly after the killing of the apostle James (the brother of John).

Obviously, King Herod Agrippa waited until this time because more Jews were in the city than usual at Passover and his actions would instill great fear in the fledgling band of believers.  But earnest prayer (verse 12) was made for Peter that greatly affected the outcome of these events.

The angel of God had to awaken a sleeping Peter, and then his chains fell off.  The angel spoke to him, *"Get up quickly...gird yourself and put on your sandals...Wrap your cloak around you and follow me,"* (verses 7-8). Then, prison doors instantly opened as Peter followed the angel. The apostle thought he was having a vision, but then finally realized what had happened (verse 11).

When Peter arrived at the home of John Mark's mother where the prayer meeting was underway, the servant girl, Rhoda, who came to the door, was so overjoyed; she ran back and announced his arrival. The believers, who had been gathered in prayer, responded strangely. *"It is his angel,"* she was told (verse 15).

I believe that angelic manifestations were common in the First Century. These early believers don't appear to be startled about this story of Peter's release through angelic intervention. It leads one to believe the appearance of an angel was more commonplace in those days.

### Numbers of Angels

Scripturally, there are nearly 300 references to angels in the Bible, and interestingly, there are more references to angels in the New Testament (about 165 occasions) than the Old Testament (where more than 100 listings occur). The mention of angels is not relegated to a few books of the Bible, but they are found in 34 books from the earliest, Genesis, to the last, Revelation.

Just how many angels there are has been a question debated by theologians since Bible days. In an answer to this question, King David wrote: *"The chariots of God are myriads, thousands upon*

79

*thousands,"* (Psalm 68:17).

Commenting on Psalm 68:17, Matthew Henry says, "Angels are 'the chariots of God,' His chariots of war, which He makes use of against His enemies, His chariots of conveyance, which He sends for His friends, as He did for Elijah... His chariots of state, in the midst of which He shows His glory and power. They are vastly numerous: 'Twenty thousands' even thousands multiplied."

By any count, the angelic company or host is enormous. Hebrews 12:22 (NKJV) calls the number *"an innumerable company of angels"*. The Amplified Bible records that same verse as *"countless multitudes of angels in festal gathering."*

In his vision on the Isle of Patmos that became the Book of Revelation, the apostle John records a scene of angels worshipping the Lord Jesus:

> *I looked and heard the voice of many angels, numbering thousands upon thousands, and ten thousand times ten thousand. They circled the throne and the living creatures and the elders. In a loud voice they sang: "Worthy is the Lamb, who was slain, to receive power and wealth and wisdom and strength and honor and glory and praise."* (Revelation 5:11-12 NIV).

"Ten thousand times ten thousand" describes some 100 million angels surrounding Jesus on the throne. This angelic company is described as "myriads of myriads" according to the NASB's rendering of Revelation 5:11.

Although theological opinions vary on the number of angels, the Bible is not specific on this subject. Revelation 19:14 states that "armies of angels" or "armies in heaven" will return with the Lord Jesus at the battle of Armageddon.

### A Ministry of Comfort & Strength

It has been stated that Psalm 103:20-21 contains an explanation of the fivefold ministry of angels. *"Bless the Lord, you His angels, mighty in strength, who perform His word, obeying the voice of His Word! Bless the Lord, all you His hosts, you who serve Him, doing His will."*

In looking at this passage, I believe these verses show God's purpose for angels, existing to serve Him in five different functions as well as blessing and worshipping the Lord. The other five purposes listed here appear to be directly linked to the roles of angels sent to minister in the believer's lives (Hebrews 1:14):

(1) They are mighty in strength; (2) they perform His Word; (3) they obey the voice of His Word; (4) they serve Him; and (5) they do His will.

In at least two places in the New Testament— Matthew 4:11 and Luke 22:43—the Bible speaks about the angels of God ministering to our own Savior. It is obvious from reading these passages that angels had a role in the ministry of Jesus and that ministry continues to this very day in the lives of God-called ministers and, for that matter, all believers.

In Matthew 4, after fasting for forty days and nights, Jesus faced temptations from Satan himself. Obviously weary from his days of fasting and his encounter with the tempter, Jesus needed the ministry of angels. *"Then the devil left Him; and behold, angels came and began to minister to Him,"* (verse 11).

*The Spirit Filled Life Bible* takes note of the Greek word *angelos* in Matthew 4:11. "From *angello*, 'to deliver a message'; hence, a messenger. In the NT the word has the special sense of a spiritual, heavenly personage attendant upon God and functioning as a messenger from the Lord sent to earth to execute His purposes and to make them known to men."

In Luke 22, Jesus walked to the Mount of Olives with his disciples for a special time of prayer before his arrest and ultimate crucifixion. The Bible describes the agony of that moment: *"...and His sweat became like drops of blood, falling down upon the ground,"* (verse 44).

In verse 43, we are told: *"Now an angel from heaven appeared to Him, strengthening Him."*

If our own Lord faced battles upon this earth requiring the angels to provide ministry and strength, how much more would you and I need this same kind of help and intervention?

## The Ministry Of Angels

Let me share a story about my own family.

My father, Harmon Oates, had a profound and lasting impact upon my life for the Lord. He was a devoted Christian, always involved in his local church and serving in various community outreaches to touch the lives of those in need. He had also been involved in former pro-football player Bill Glass's Prison Ministry, and was on the Board of Inmate Encounter, a Florida based prison ministry.

After a long bout with emphysema, Dad went home to be with the Lord. Before his death, he asked me to conduct his funeral, and I knew I had a difficult task ahead. How does a pastor handle the funeral of his own father without falling apart? I really wasn't sure I could handle the service.

After giving some introductory remarks, I was overcome with emotion and not sure I could continue. My brother, Charles, read some of Dad's favorite Bible passages while I took a seat and tried to compose myself. "I don't know if I can make it through this, Lord," I prayed. "I really need some help."

Then, I looked down the center aisle and saw an angel standing there. In fact, he appeared to be a junior version of an angel I had seen in Manaus, Brazil several weeks before. As I looked closer, I saw angels standing shoulder to shoulder around the entire room and all were holding drawn swords.

That changed me right on the spot! I knew that God's Presence was in that place and everything was going to be okay. My super-charged emotions became settled as the peace of God flooded my being. Strength immediately came to me as I stood and began to minister in the power of God's Spirit to my father's family and friends gathered.

The Lord alone knew I needed the strength and encouragement of His angels. It brought to mind the words of Psalm 91:11-12, *"For He will give His angels charge concerning you, to guard you in all your ways. They will bear you up in their hands, that you do not strike your foot against a stone."* ·

In describing Psalm 91:11-12, Dr. Billy Graham believes that each of us has our own private guardian angels. Observing the plural *"angels"* in this text, he has concluded that each believer must have at least two angels whose assigned duty is to protect them.

### The Angels & Healing

John 5:1-4 tells a story about the pool of Bethesda in Jerusalem where the work of an angel produces healing on the part of those sick people who enter the water.

> *In these lay a multitude of those who were sick, blind, lame, and withered, waiting for the moving of the waters;*
> *For an angel of the Lord went down at certain seasons into the pool and stirred up the water; whoever then first, after the stirring up of the water, stepped in was made well from whatever disease*

*with which he was afflicted,* (verses 3-4).

The glory of God fell in services one day in Maua, a suburban city of Sao Paulo, Brazil, similar to the account of 1 Kings 8:11 where *"the priests could not stand to minister because of the cloud, for the glory of the Lord filled the house of the Lord."* No one could stand up in Maua, either.

That day I was preaching on the subject of "The Glory of God" when the power came. People started crying. Some fell to the floor. My interpreter dropped to the floor, her glasses hanging off her face. The microphone had rolled out of her hand.

The church's pastor came forward and tried to revive her without any success. Another interpreter came forward while I silently prayed what to do. "Do nothing," the Lord instructed me. "Watch what I'm going to do."

Another wave came through the room more intense than the first. The third wave that came through was so intense and thick I could not stand. I was somewhat stretched out with my arms holding onto the podium but my feet were like lead. I couldn't move my legs to keep me from falling, and I started sliding down the podium. I lay on the floor over an hour and a half.

The pastor and all five of his assistants were on the floor. The meeting was left completely in God's hands. People were crying out. Tears flowed freely. Many were on their faces as pockets of God's glory touched people in various parts of the building.

The results of God's glory falling in a service are always healing, miracles, signs and wonders. We didn't know until the next day what the Lord had done. Then, the healing testimonies poured into us. One man, age 25, and deaf in one ear was healed instantly when his ear popped open. A woman said her eyes began to burn and then three angels came and touched her eyes. She didn't need glasses anymore; she could see perfectly.

Another woman had a hole in her forearm where a disease had eaten away the flesh. God did a creative miracle giving her new muscle and new flesh. No one ever prayed for any of these people.

In meetings in Rio, I saw a woman standing (like a statue) near Kathi. The woman was perfectly still except her left arm was moving around and occasionally her face would grimace in pain. "I'm not doing that," she repeated. "I'm not doing that."

As it turned out, the woman had been born through a botched forceps delivery causing her left arm and shoulder to become impaired and shorter than the right. Kathi watched as an angel of the Lord began twisting and moving the woman's arm. Her shoulder started filling out, her arm lengthened and her mobility was restored.

A Brazilian pastor stood watching the whole prayer time Kathi had with the young woman as she prayed for the girl's hand, arm and shoulder. The next night he came asking us a question through our interpreter. "What's the relationship with angels and healing?" he asked. "I saw the angel manipulating that girl's arm."

Without question, angels are involved in many supernatural healings.

At Global Awakening's Harrisburg conference in 2003, Kathi began praying over people when she noticed an angel standing behind a man. She touched the man's head and he fell down vibrating violently across a chair. It seemed a line formed immediately for Kathi to pray in the midst of all the angelic activity.

Finally, the man calmed down and Kathi saw the angel blow on the man's head three times. She didn't know what was wrong with the man but—agreeing with the angel's actions—she did exactly as she had seen the angel do, and blew three times on the man's head. After some time, Kathi asked, "What's been wrong with you?"

"It's kinda hard to explain," the man replied, "but I had electric shock treatment three years ago. They scrambled my brain and I lost who I was. When you put your hands on my head, I felt my brain cells being rearranged. I feel like I've gotten my personhood back."

### The Wings of Angels

In Isaiah 6:1-6, the prophet describes a scene in which he has a vision of the Lord on His throne with six-winged seraphim worshipping above the throne. *"Seraphim stood above Him, each having six wings: with two he covered his face, and with two he covered his feet, and with two he flew"*, (verse two).

In commenting on this passage, *the Spirit Filled Life Bible* says: "The ministry of the seraphim is closely related to the throne and the praises of God. They are seen constantly glorifying God— extolling His nature and attributes, and apparently supervising heaven's worship. It is possible the seraphim are the praising angels of Psalm 148:2 though they are not specifically identified as such."

Seraphim is the plural of the Hebrew *seraph*, and is identified as a burning, fiery, gliding, angelic being. It has been suggested the seraphim may be angels of a fiery color or appearance or flame-like in motion or clearness.

Obviously, the seraphim have a role in praising the Name and character of God in heaven. But Isaiah 6:6-7 leads us to believe they also have a role to cleanse and purify the servants of the Lord. *"Then one of the seraphim flew to me with a burning coal in his hand, which he had taken from the altar with tongs. He touched my mouth with it and said, 'Behold, this has touched your lips; and your iniquity is taken away, and your sin is forgiven'."*

During several angelic encounters, I experienced being wrapped in angels' wings. But shortly after my father's funeral, I had a similar experience while praying over my mother, Ruby Oates. They had been married well over sixty years and now she was going to be alone.  Most of her offspring lived in distant cities.

Mom and I were both weeping the day I prayed for her, but strangely, as I prayed, I saw an angel come up behind her and hold her in his wings.  An overwhelming peace in God's ability to care for my mother swept over me.  "Mom, the Lord has sent His angel, and you're in good hands," I told her.

About six weeks later when Kathi and I visited, she said, "I have something to tell you.  I was real tired the other day and I took a brief nap.  As I was coming out of sleep and ready to get up, I noticed a bright light arched over me.  I looked and then it disappeared."

I smiled.  "I believe that was God's way of showing you He's sent an angel to take care of you," I suggested.

"I believe it too," she replied confidently.

Speaking of "wings" or "feathers" may sound farfetched for some people but there is Bible evidence for it.  Psalm 91:4 says in the New King James Version: *"He shall cover you with His feathers, and under His wings you shall take refuge; His truth shall be your shield and buckler."*

Bible teacher Marilyn Hickey observes the following about Psalm 91:4, "Since God has no feathers or wings, some have suggested that these feathers and wings speak of our guardian angels' wings, which protectively cover us to keep us from falling, getting lost, or stumbling into unknown dangers in the unseen realm of the spirit."

## Angels and the Fire of God

This brilliant color or glory of the seraphim (also described by Ezekiel of the four living creatures) is a picture as well of the angel who came from heaven and rolled away the stone from the sepulcher where Jesus was buried. Matthew describes the angel in this manner:

> *And his appearance was like lightning, and his clothing as white as snow,* (Matthew 28:3).

Matthew's description of the angel agrees with the words of Daniel 10:6 where the prophet had been seeking the Lord for three full weeks. *"His body also was like beryl, his face had the appearance of lightning, his eyes were like flaming torches, his arms and feet like the gleam of polished bronze, and the sound of his words like the sound of a tumult."*

Also, the writer of Hebrews connects with this picture of fire and brilliance in the angel's appearance. *"And of the angels He says: Who makes His angels wind and His ministers a flame of fire"* (Hebrews 1:7). In a similar way, 2 Thessalonians 1:7 states *"...the Lord Jesus will be revealed from heaven with His mighty angels in flaming fire."*

This "white and dazzling as lightning" appearance is further confirmed by General William Booth, who founded the Salvation Army. He wrote about a vision of angelic beings, stating that every angel was surrounded with an aurora of rainbow light so brilliant that were it not withheld, no human being could stand the sight.

## An Experience in Brazil

In Manaus, Brazil where we were holding services, the church suddenly began erupting with the Presence of God. Right behind where our ministry team was seated, pockets of God's glory were touching an entire section of people. I didn't see angels ministering to the people but I saw the affect of the angels' ministry.

I walked over to the ministry team and announced, "Turn around and look behind you." It was so noisy in the building nobody but a girl named Rachel Stoppard even looked. The following are her exact words of what she saw:

"I turned around slowly and what I saw first were chariots of fire all along the back wall. As I followed this around, I glimpsed a huge angel standing behind me and suddenly fire was shooting out of him. It so caught me off guard that I fell into a chair but the angel caught me.

"As he did, this fire shot from him into me starting at my head. It was like electric waves of fire in my head proceeding on down to my arms and to my legs. It was like wave after wave of this slowly pulsating through my body. I wanted to scream because I thought I was going to die as this fire went through me.

"As a wave would go through, I could feel the angel's arms around me tightening up and saying, 'just relax. I've got you. You're not going to die.' He held me and kept saying, 'I'm not leaving...I'm not leaving.'

"In the process of all this happening, I started becoming aware out ahead in the distance I could see the throne room. As I started focusing on the throne, I began crying, 'Take me...I want to go there. I want to go there.' I could see the soft light pulsating off the throne and I could see the colors swirling and moving.

"Finally, the angel said, 'no, it's not time yet. You are to stay here.' Gradually, the picture before me began to fade and I became aware about four hours had passed. Since then, I have cried out for a renewed intimacy with God.

"It was at this point I became aware that my husband, Gary, and I have a call to the nations. I was aware there is a place in the throne room where prayers and intercession are released so that the coals of fire can be taken to the nations. I also came to realize that this fire is taken into families and passed from fathers and mothers to their children."

### Seeing Angels First-Hand

In his classic book on *Angels: God's Secret Agents*, famed evangelist Billy Graham writes that he can't say that he has ever seen an angel although he believes their biblical role in our lives. That would probably be the majority opinion of most Christians.

Scholars have debated whether or not the expression "sons of God" in Genesis 6:2 refers to angels. However, Scripture is emphatic that angels are ministering "spirits" (Hebrews 1:14), and thus are non-material. Angels do not possess physical bodies, but they may take on such bodies if appointed to a special task by the Lord.

The writer of Hebrews further confirms that angels may have a physical appearance we wouldn't recognize. *"Do not neglect to show hospitality to strangers, for by this some have entertained angels without knowing it,"* (Hebrews 13:2).

Yet, the Bible itself gives us examples of those who *actually* had their eyes opened to see angels. Let me cite three obvious examples. The first is found in Numbers 22:22-30 where the prophet Balaam has been recruited from Mesopotamia by the Moabites to come and curse the nation of Israel. On his way with the princes of Moab, the Angel of the Lord blocks Balaam's path. Amazingly, Balaam's donkey saw the angel first!

*"Then the Lord opened the eyes of Balaam, and* **he saw the angel of the Lord** *standing in the way with His drawn sword in His hand; and he bowed all the way to the ground,"* (Numbers 22:31, *author's emphasis*).

Even though he was a prophet and should have been the one to see the Angel of the Lord, Balaam had no such vision until the Lord opened his eyes. What did Balaam see? Obviously, Balaam saw the physical appearance of an angel and carried on a conversation with him (verses 32-35).

Our second example of a person's eyes being opened to see an angel is found in 2 Samuel 24 where David has sinned against the Lord by *"numbering the people"* (verse 10). The prophet Gad then brings David a choice of three punishments for his sin (verse 13).

Scripture records that a "destroying angel" was sent with a plague and seventy thousand men of the people died. *"And the Angel of the Lord was by the threshing floor of Araunah the Jebusite"* (verse 16).

The next verse describes something incredible happening to David. *"Then David spoke to the Lord when **he saw the angel** who was striking down the people..."* (verse 17, *author's emphasis*).

David *saw* the angel. He became visible—and very few people can ever be the same again after being confronted with one of God's supernatural beings!

King David became deeply penitent, *"...Behold, it is I who have sinned, and it is I who have done wrong; but these sheep, what have they done? Please let Your hand be against me and against my father's house"* (verse 17).

Interestingly, the threshing floor of Araunah was on Mt. Moriah where Abraham offered Isaac

(Genesis 22:2), and later the location of Solomon's temple (2 Chronicles 3:1).

Our third example is found in 2 Kings 6 where the king of Syria is waging war against Israel but God is giving strategies to the prophet Elisha in order to defeat the invading forces. Horses and chariots and a great army come by night and surround the city of Dothan where Elisha resides (verse 13-14).

At daybreak, Elisha's servant is confronted with the problem. *"Alas, my master! What shall we do?"* he asks the prophet (verse 15).

Elisha's answer is filled with confidence in God. *"Do not fear, for those who are with us are more than those who are with them"* (verse 16).

Then the prophet prays an unusual prayer: *"'O Lord, I pray, open his eyes that he may see.' And the Lord opened the servant's eyes and **he saw**; and behold, the mountain was full of horses and chariots of fire all around Elisha"* (verse 17, *author's emphasis*).

Obviously, these spirit beings or angels were there before the servant's eyes were opened. However, they were unseen by natural eyes, and only after Elisha's prayer were "spiritual eyes" opened to see these beings sent from heaven.

In studying 2 Kings 6:17, it is obvious this is an example of natural men being granted insight into the unseen world of spirit beings. The chariots and horses could not be seen by the naked eye until God had answered Elisha's prayer. Then, the spirit beings (who had been there all the time) were completely visible.

It not only happened in Elisha's day. It's happening today!

### New Testament Examples

Someone might suggest that the Scriptures we just reviewed of Bible characters seeing angels face to face were all from the Old Testament. That is exactly correct. However, the following five examples of angelic activity all come from the New Testament.

Our first example is found in Luke 1:11-22 where Zacharias (soon-to-be the father of John the Baptist) is given that news by the angel Gabriel *"who stands in the presence of God"* (verse 19).

The significant passage for our study is in Luke 1:11-12 (*author's emphasis*), which says, *"And an angel of the Lord **appeared to him**, standing to the right of the altar of incense. And Zacharias was troubled when he **saw him**, and fear gripped him."*

Notice that Zacharais *saw* the angel of God!

Our second example of angelic visitation in Luke 1:26-38 announces to the virgin Mary the coming birth of Jesus who *"will be called the Son of the Most High; and the Lord God will give Him the throne of His father David"* (verse 32).

That announcement also comes from the

angel Gabriel who has been dispatched to Nazareth to bring the news to Mary. There is no question that she saw the angel because she carried on a conversation with him.

In this case of an angel appearing to humans, Mary speaks with Gabriel about our Lord's birth. She is reminded about her relative Elizabeth who "also conceived a son in her old age; and she who was barren is now in her sixth month" (verse 36), and "nothing will be impossible with God" (verse 37). Then, the angel departs.

Our third example is located in John 20:11-12 where Mary Magdalene has discovered Jesus' burial tomb is now empty of His body. *"But Mary was standing outside the tomb weeping; and so, as she wept, she stooped and looked into the tomb; and **she saw two angels** in white sitting, one at the head and one at the feet, where the body of Jesus had been lying,"* (author's emphasis).

Some Bible translations state that Mary "beheld" the angels, which is an archaic way of saying she "saw" them. It is quite clear Mary Magdalene saw the two angels! They were for real and, indeed, she carried on a conversation with them (verse 13).

Our fourth case is described in Acts 12:4-11 where the apostle Peter has been arrested and is being guarded by four squads or sixteen solders. Yet, the angel of the Lord shows up in the cell, wakes up a sleeping Peter bound with two chains, and they walk out as prison doors open and chains fall off.

Peter thought he was having a vision (verse nine), but that all changed when he found himself set free and the angel departed. *"When Peter came to himself, he said, 'Now I know for sure that the Lord has sent forth His angel and rescued me from the hand of Herod and from all that the Jewish people were expecting,"* (Acts 12:11).

Our fifth example is found in Acts 27:23-24 where the angel of the Lord appears on board a storm-tossed ship carrying the apostle Paul to Rome. Paul's encouragement to those on board is simple.

> *"For this very night an angel of the God to whom I belong and whom I serve* **stood before me,** *saying 'Do not be afraid, Paul; you must stand before Caesar; and behold, God has granted you all those who are sailing with you',"* (*author's emphasis*).

Paul agrees with what he's been told by the angel. He says *"...It will turn out exactly as I have been told,"* (verse 25).

## Signs, Wonders & Angels

In September 2002, Kathi and I joined another Global Awakening mission trip to Brazil beginning in the tropical city of Manaus, which had strangely not had rain in three months. Randy Clark had asked me to do the morning teaching session, and one morning, I gave my testimony of angelic visitations.

# The Ministry Of Angels

As the ministry time began, I saw three angels ministering to a woman in the congregation. I walked over to her and pointed out what I saw happening. As I spoke, the Spirit of the Lord came upon the woman and she began to weep.

I walked back to the center of the stage and glanced down the church's center aisle. Standing in the middle of the aisle was a huge angel, at least thirty feet tall, holding an extremely large sword in his right hand. His appearance—both overwhelming and unbelievable to behold—was that of a Roman gladiator. I knew immediately he was a war angel.

I raised my right hand and pointed at the angel. "There's an angel," I tried to say; although I'm not sure I got all the words out. At that moment, a gust of wind came from the angel that blew across me and I fell down backwards on the platform. It wasn't that the wind was so strong to blow anyone down; it was the Presence of the Lord in the wind. I simply couldn't stand.

Behind the platform was an archway with two gold doors. The doors blew open with that wind. Plants on the stage were shaking in the breeze. I was lying there on the floor holding the microphone but I couldn't move. I was speechless.

Randy, sitting on the front row, looked over at Kathi, and said, "You take over."

She came up, took the microphone out of my hand and began to prophesy: "the wind of the Holy

Spirit is going to blow through Brazil...and the foreign gods of Brazil will be no more...Our Lord is the one true God and He will establish His lordship in Brazil."

As she waved her hand towards the congregation, several rows of white plastic chairs in the back blew over. A man stepped outside the building to see if the wind was blowing outside but it wasn't. The trees were not blowing. It was perfectly still.

Inside, the wind was whipping around just like on the day of Pentecost—a mighty rushing wind had come into the house. The angelic activity was obvious in that sanctuary. They were swirling all over the place. I was eventually able to crawl around on the floor, get the microphone and release the ministry team. Team members would later talk of strong winds blowing in a circular motion around them as they ministered. Reports would also come back that virtually everyone prayed over that day was instantly healed.

As I was trying to get up, I felt a mist come over my face. It was like the glory cloud of God had come down, and I could physically feel the mist coming over me. Later, I could even smell the incense of the Lord.

That church—one of the largest in Brazil with a membership exceeding 48,000—was leveled with the Presence of God. People were either on the floor weeping as the Lord moved among us, or standing awestruck with hands raised in worship and praise.

My point is that God uses His angels to perform His works, and signs and wonders. He used the natural elements in manifesting His Presence and glory in that church.

## Traveling with Angels

Some weeks ago before traveling to the Ukraine, we sent out a prayer letter. Included in that prayer letter was a request that our luggage would be safe and not arrive damaged. Since we were traveling from one continent to another...that's important.

The day we left the USA, Kathi and I were standing at the airport watching our plane being loaded. As I watched the luggage being carried up a conveyor belt into the jet, the Lord suddenly opened my eyes.

I saw an angel sitting on each of our bags! And just before the bags disappeared into the airplane, the angel on the first bag waved at me and smiled. What comfort and peace—needless to say— our luggage arrived safely at our destination!

## Questions & Answers

Frequently, I'm asked questions about some of my experiences, and I'd like to address a few of those inquiries.

**Q.** Do you see angels all the time?

**A.**  No.  There are times that God opens my eyes to see the angels at the most unsuspecting time. It seems that occurs when I would least expect to see anything and He suddenly opens my eyes.  There are other times when I'd expect to see all kinds of stuff but I don't see anything.  The more sensitive I am to the Presence of God, it seems the more I am able to see in the realm of the Spirit.

**Q.**  Do I see angels like I see others?

**A.**  Most of the time, no.  I see them through the eye of my spirit.  I see them as if they are transparent, and I can see right through them.  Most of the time I see them with my eyes open instead of closed.  I can see how they're dressed and what they're doing.  I can see all of that as if they're transparent.  I have also seen them when it was just like looking at another person.  At times, I have seen them as flames of fire, or columns of light.  I have also seen parts of their bodies.

**Q.**  Does seeing in the realm of the Spirit mean that I will see the demonic as well?

**A.**  Seeing in the realm of the Spirit is also a type of the gift of discerning of spirits (1 Corinthians 12:10).  With the discernment, one will be able to distinguish between the realm of God and the realm of the satanic.  But don't be afraid if you see a demon.  Ask God why He allowed you to see a demon.  Remember we have power and authority over evil spirits.

102

**Q.** Are angels to be worshipped?

**A.** No. Angels are not to be worshipped. Revelation 22:8-9 is very clear on this point. "And I, John, am the one who heard and saw these things. And when I heard and saw, I fell down to worship at the feet of the angel who showed me these things. And he said to me, 'Do not do that; I am a fellow servant of yours and of your brethren the prophets and of those who heed the words of this book; worship God'."

The answer is abundantly clear. Worship God and Him alone!

**Q.** Does the manifestation of angels in a believer's life diminish the role of the Holy Spirit?

**A.** Absolutely not. The angels are "ministering spirits" (Hebrews 1:14) who serve the will and purpose of Almighty God. The angels would not function in any manner contrary to the Spirit's directions. They are merely carrying out the ministry of the Holy Spirit in our lives.

## Chapter 6

# TRUE INTIMACY WITH GOD

*"Revival breaks out when people are desperate for God. When they become intimate with Him and lose sight of themselves, then anything can happen."*

—Rolland Baker from *Charisma*, March 2004.

We need to remember that God created us in His likeness and image so that we can have intimacy and relationship with Him. Often we are so busy seeking an experience or the gifts, or wanting more of His power.

The truth is: we're not seeking the face of God. We have not developed an intimate relationship with Him that He longs for and which we so desperately need.

His desire for us is—us!

Did you know that God placed in our DNA a hunger, a thirst and a desire for more of Him? He created us with a passion to know Him. If we're not experiencing that burning desire, then we have allowed other things to get in the way. "Other things"—job, family, bills, and hobbies—all have a way of crowding out the central focus of our lives.

In Jeremiah 24:7, the Bible gives us a picture of our creation by Almighty God,

> *"I will give them a heart to know Me,*
> *for I am the Lord; and they will be My*
> *people, and I will be their God..."*

As my friend, Bill Johnson, Pastor of Bethel Church in Redding, California has often said, "I didn't marry my wife so we could correspond by e-mail. I didn't marry her so we could talk on the phone. I married her because I wanted to be with her. I enjoy her presence. I'm not interested in telling people about the theology of my wife, or explaining that she exists, or how much I believe in her. I like her to be with me. I love her presence."

In a similar way, God has placed in our hearts a desire for more of Him. You don't necessarily need a better theological understanding of the Lord. You need to *experience* the true intimate Presence of the living God. That will radically change your life.

The Presence of God is available to every child

of the King. In that light, our Savior makes a wonderful promise in John 14:21 about how He is revealed or manifested through a life of obedience to Him. *"He who has My commandments and keeps them is the one who loves Me; and he who loves Me will be loved by My Father, and I will love him and will disclose Myself to him."*

The Amplified Bible opens John 14:21 with even greater understanding. Listen to these words (*author's emphasis*):

> *"The person who has My commands and keeps them is the one who [really] loves Me; and whoever [really] loves Me will be loved by My Father, and I [too] will love him and will* **show (reveal, manifest)** *Myself to him. [I will let Myself be* **clearly seen** *by him and make Myself* **real** *to him.]"*

The Lord Jesus has promised to reveal Himself to those who are obedient. In fact, two other verses—John 14:15 and John 14:23—confirm that God is looking for a particular level of obedience from His children.

> *"If you love Me, you will keep My commandments,"* (John 14:15).

> *Jesus answered and said to him, "If anyone loves Me, he will keep My Word; and My Father will love him, and we will come to him and make Our abode with him,"* (John 14:23).

When Jesus says the same thing three times in eight verses of Scripture (verses 15-23), I think it's important that we pay attention. I believe He wants us to get the message about obedience.

If I asked the typical church audience if they love Jesus, virtually everyone would say "yes". Yet Jesus says, if you love Me, you will do what I say. The demonstration of love is obedience, and obedience has the capacity of causing you to live differently in the eyes of the world. We are to be called to be a peculiar people—and obedience to God will set you apart from others in the crowd.

A short time ago Kathi and I were attempting to help a woman through some serious issues in her life. One night we had to go into a bar and bring her home. "Well, you know," she said drunkenly, "I love Jesus."

Yet, Jesus makes the issue plain: If you love Me, you will obey Me!

Our obedience is the way we tell Jesus that we truly love Him. In verse 21, He promises to be clearly seen by those who obey. The Amplified Bible uses words like "show", "reveal", and "manifest". Obedient people will have a first-hand relationship with the living God.

Have you experienced the reality of God in your life? Do you want God to become more real to you? How does all of this happen?

In my own life I know that I took a major turn when I simply took off my shoes to stand on a dirty concrete floor in a Brazilian church in June 2002. I have never been the same since that small act of obedience to the Lord.

Yet, God requires obedience in small things before He ever entrusts greater things to us. I have now been entrusted with a ministry where I see God opening blind eyes, deaf ears are healed, cancers fall off, tumors disappear, and people come out of wheelchairs.

Obedience to God is one of the keys that has opened my life to seeing the Book of Acts being repeated around the world. And I am convinced, it would have never occurred without a higher level of obedience.

## A Word from Heaven

In December 2002 while we were holding services in Joao Pessao, Brazil, one of the team members—Rick Sodmont from Pennsylvania—came up on the platform to give a word of knowledge. When he stepped to the microphone, the power of God moved into the room in an overwhelming way.

Rick never actually gave the word. Instead, he fell onto the floor under the power of the Lord and wound up there for almost an hour. When he finally stood, he was shaking and trembling. In fact, for a while I thought the platform was actually vibrating because of all that God was in the midst of doing.

When I spoke with him later, he told me that he had been taken up into the Presence of the Lord where two large chains holding a chest full of garbage had been cut off his back by a sword. "The Lord cut the chains across my shoulders with the sword and the chest fell off my back," Rick explained. "I felt a tremendous relief from the weight and bondage removed that I had carried all of my life."

Then, two angels took and washed him from the dirt and debris left on his back in a waterfall flowing with rivers of water. Then he was brought back into God's Presence. The Lord told him to come back to earth and bring a message. Here is part of the message:

"This is the message that I want you to tell My people. Tell them to wake up. Tell them to wake up because many in my church are sleeping. There are many who go through the motions but few have entered into intimacy and relationship with Me. **What I desire above all things is to have an intimate relationship with each of you. Out of that intimacy, I will empower you** and send you out to reach those who need Jesus Christ. The quicker you enter into this relationship the quicker you will be empowered and sent forth. The quicker you do this the world will be won and then I will come and take you home. Those who **choose** to enter into that intimacy now, I will come and fellowship with them and be intimate with them even now. That is the message I have for My people to enter into intimacy through relationship...." (*author's emphasis*).

This is a message straight from the heavenly Father. God wants intimacy with us. He loves our presence. His priority is to have intimacy with us, and the bi-product of that intimacy is empowerment. Notice that it's a choice that we make to enter into this intimacy. *"Draw near to God and He will draw near to you..."* (James 4:8).

Notice also that we take the first step!

How much effort are we willing to make in seeking Him? I hear people say they prayed and nothing happened. But often times, it's a feeble attempt. Some are looking for instant results and when that doesn't happen, they quit. Instant results may not happen, but I encourage you to be diligent in your pursuit of the living God and become intimate with Him.

### Elijah & Elisha

In 2 Kings 2:9, Elisha wanted a double portion of the anointing that functioned upon his mentor, Elijah. Elijah's response to that request: *"You have asked a hard thing. Nevertheless, if you see me when I am taken from you, it shall be so for you; but if not, it shall not be so,"* (verse 10).

What did Elisha do?

He wouldn't let Elijah out of his sight. If the prophet went from Gilgal to Bethel, Elisha was right there. If he traveled to Jericho, or down to the Jordan River, Elisha stood nearby. He was unyielding in pursuit of that double portion on his life. He was not giving up. He stuck like chewing gum on the bottom of Elijah's shoe!

The result of Elisha's pursuit of that double portion is clear according to 2 Kings 2:15. *Now when the sons of the prophets who were from Jericho saw him, they said, "The spirit of Elijah rests on Elisha..."*

Because we truly want God's highest and best for our lives, then we should be willing to make sacrifice to receive. It is obvious that Elisha experienced Elijah's anointing only because he was willing to pay a price to receive. The examples of Scripture are abundantly clear in this regard. We will never receive from heaven without sacrifice or a willingness to pay a price.

### Jacob & the Angel

In Genesis 32, we read of Jacob wrestling with the angel. The angel of the Lord was getting tired of the wrestling match but Jacob wasn't letting go. *"I will not let You go unless You bless me!"* declared Jacob (verse 26).

In essence, Jacob was saying: "I'm not stopping anything short of the fullest blessing of God." He was unyielding and wrestled all night.

Jacob demonstrated a willingness to contend with God at a time of desperate need in his life. The result was even a name change for Jacob. The angel of God announced: *"...Your name shall no longer be Jacob, but Israel; for you have striven with God and with men, and have prevailed,"* (verse 28).

Jacob's name had meant "Supplanter" or "Deceiver", but now he would be called Israel, which can mean "Prince with God" or "He Strives with God" or "May God Persevere". Hosea 12:2-6 later points to Jacob as an example to be followed when one is in the midst of a struggle or a need for character change.

Genesis 32:30 tells us: *"So Jacob named the place Peniel, for he said, 'I have seen God face to face, yet my life has been preserved'."*

Jacob was seeking with all his might and found the face of God. He was not willing to give up. The struggle produced something heavenly in Jacob. His life was never the same after the encounter with the angel of the Lord. He found strength he didn't know he had. He was transformed.

### Jesus & the Disciples

In Mark 6:45-52, the disciples are in their boat in the middle of the sea and the winds are suddenly coming up. Where is Jesus? He's up in the mountains praying but He's not in the dark. He sees the disciples and knows exactly what's going on. In verse 48 (*author's emphasis*), I recently discovered a part of that passage I'd never seen before.

> *Seeing them straining at the oars, for the wind was against them, at about the fourth watch of the night He came to them, walking on the sea; and He*

113

*intended* to pass by them.

His intent was to walk right pass them. His intent was not to help them. Why was that? He wanted them to cry out for His help; He wanted them to seek Him.

But when they cried out to Jesus, everything changed. *"...But immediately He spoke with them and said to them, 'Take courage; it is I, do not be afraid'. And He got into the boat with them, and the wind stopped; and they were greatly astonished,"* (verses 50-51).

When we've tried everything else and exhausted our natural resources, we finally yield and call out to Him. Jesus was right there beside the boat and would have continued walking unless they had cried out to Him.

The same is true in our lives each day. Jesus is right there waiting for us to cry out for more of Him. God wants us to seek His face with all of our hearts--giving Him our all.

2 Chronicles 16:9 tells us something important about how God is searching for us: *"For the eyes of the Lord move to and fro throughout the earth that He may strongly support those whose heart is completely His..."*

Why is God doing this? What's His purpose?

God is looking for people whose heart belongs to Him alone. He's going throughout the earth. That makes it sound as if there are not that many people out there whose heart is completely His. He's searching. He's looking all over. He's looking for people He can bless and support. He's looking for people who are hungry for intimacy with Him and willing to abandon all.

David makes a solemn request in Psalm 86:11 (NIV), *"Teach me Your way, O Lord, and I will walk in Your truth; give me an undivided hear, that I may fear Your name."*

A divided heart can keep us out of God's Presence. It seems that many want to keep one foot in the world and another foot in the church. That's a divided heart and it will not work.

This is all about complete surrender. It's a call to 100 percent commitment to Him. It's saying to the Lord: "I want everything You've got. I'll pay whatever the price. I want intimacy with You!"

### An Obstacle to Intimacy

Recently, I received an e-mail from a friend who writes about an obstacle to intimacy that she experienced when a separation occurred in a relationship with her best friend.

"In my quiet times, I often ask the Lord to search my heart to see if there is any offensive way in me and to give me an undivided heart that I may fear His Name...The Lord has faithfully honored my request in the past but I was totally unprepared for what He was about to show me this time.

"I was feeling rejection and abandonment because of this separation taking place in this friendship. I wanted to see a Christian counselor but after calling several, I discovered they were all booked up. I called some fiends who could really hear from God but they were out of town. It seemed God had removed all human influence from me so I was left to depend upon Him alone.

"That evening, I began reading a book that contained a section on codependency. It was then the Holy Spirit convicted me of trying to be God in this other person's life. He also convicted me of other sins. Yet, I knew God wasn't finished with me.

"In a time of quietness with the Lord, I sensed His Presence near. 'You have asked many times for more of Me and more power in your life, but you've never asked why you haven't received. I said, 'No, Lord. Why?'

"He then lovingly said 'Because there has been no room at the inn. You have allowed this friendship to take My place in your heart. That's why I've brought all of this about to show you I am jealous for you. I want all of your heart, an undivided heart that you may know Me'."

This e-mail from my friend is really from the heart of God expressing what He wants from each of us—an undivided heart. We are to seek after more of God in our lives that we might know Him intimately.

Understanding the value of an undivided

heart, David acknowledged its merits in Psalm 27:8, *"When You said, 'Seek My face,' my heart said to You. 'Your face, O Lord, I shall seek'."*

His face is there to be sought after. When the Lord says, "seek my face", we have an important choice to make here. Our heart wants to seek the Lord; yet, our flesh will oppose us in a multitude of ways. Our heart is crying out "yes"; our flesh is screaming "no". Sadly, our flesh wins most of the time. David understood the proper response to God's command by simply following the cry of his heart.

Listen to the beautiful way Psalm 27:8 is presented in the Amplified Bible (*author's emphasis*): *"You have said, Seek My face [inquire for and require My presence as your vital need]. My **heart** says to You, Your face (Your presence), Lord, will I seek, inquire for, and require [of necessity and on the authority of Your Word]."*

This desire of seeking the face of God has been placed in all of our hearts. Our natural, fleshly man resists because he will lose his influence in our lives. Every kind of obstacle and endless distraction will come your way. Yet, it's important to follow our heart and seek the face of God, yielding to the desire God has placed in our hearts.

Jamie Buckingham once wrote: "Deep inside, all of us seem to know intuitively that until we withdraw from all we consider necessary to our comfort, we will not come face to face with God. Only in times and places of solitude do people have genuine spiritual confrontation.

117

"Perhaps it is for this reason that we fear solitude. As soon as we are alone, without people to talk to, books to read, TV to watch or phone calls to make, an inner chaos opens in us—threatening to swallow us like ships caught in a giant whirlpool. Thus, we do everything we can to keep from being alone..."

## Further Obstacles

A picture of Jesus and His church emerges from the Song of Solomon 2:8-9 using an example of the bride and the bridegroom. Listen to the heart of God speaking through these verses:

> *Listen! My beloved! Behold, he is coming, climbing on the mountains, leaping on the hills! My beloved is like a gazelle or a young stag. Behold, he is standing behind our wall, he is looking through the windows, he is peering through the lattice.*

The bridegroom—who is Jesus in this story—wants in but he's standing behind OUR WALL. He's standing behind the barrier we've erected that prevents us from experiencing intimacy with Him. The wall must come down if we are going to abide in His Presence.

A wall is anything in your life that stands between you and God. Some walls are built quickly while others occur over time as we add layer after layer. All such walls are a barrier to the power and

Presence of God working in your life. None of us can truly walk in God's will for our lives when these obstacles obstruct our pathway.

Obviously, sin is a wall, as well as past hurts. Hebrews 12:1 looks at these problems in this light: *"...let us also lay aside every encumbrance and the sin which so easily entangles us, and let us run with endurance the race that is set before us."*

Maybe you're even mad at God. He disappointed you. He let you down. Perhaps your prayer didn't get answered. God didn't do what you thought He was going to do whenever you thought He'd do it. Maybe your life is turning out a lot different than you planned.

Whatever the issue, barrier or wall, they are all designed to keep you from experiencing God's highest and best for your life.

Two years prior to our spiritual breakthrough, Kathi and I decided to get cleaned up on the inside. Outwardly, we probably looked good—almost the perfect pastor and his adoring family.

But inwardly (and behind closed doors), it was a different story. Control issues, ambitions, pride, resentments, hurts and woundedness were all lurking in the shadows. It was time to pursue God for a deep reworking of the "hidden parts" where Jesus requires truth and purity.

Deciding to face these hidden issues— honestly and forthrightly—sent us on a journey that continues to this very day. The result has been deep cleansing and healing of hurts, wounds, mindsets, motivations and ambitions. As Mike Bickle says, "Intimacy with God is about allowing the rubbish to get out so the love of God can get in."

## A Test Case

A woman came forward for prayer in one of our meetings and had a long list of problems to confront. "I'm not in touch with God," she said dejectedly. "I can't see Him, feel Him or hear Him. It seems like He's no where in my life."

"Okay, let's take a moment here," I suggested. "I want you to ask God to reveal to you what these walls are in your life." I gave her a few words of instruction and then she prayed.

After a long pause, she then began repeating a list of "walls" as God was revealing them to her: abandonment, rejection, and hurts of every kind imaginable.

"Those walls have been a protection to you," I explained. "They've become a friend seemingly protecting you from more hurt and pain."

She nodded her head. "Are you willing to ask Jesus to deal with the walls and become that wall of protection for you?" I asked.

She thought for a moment, and then slowly said "yes". She repeated a prayer with me and we waited, as the tears began streaming down her face.

"What's happening?" I questioned.

"Jesus is tearing the walls down," she answered. "He's destroying them. The walls are crumbling."

By now, she was weeping profusely. "What's happening now?" I asked.

"Jesus is coming towards me," she replied, "and He's telling me that He loves me...He's reaching out, holding me and hugging me."

In matter of minutes she went from not being "in touch" at all with God to a place of seeing, hearing and feeling His Presence.

The woman was completely set free as Jesus removed the walls. The barriers and obstacles fell as we prayed together. When the obstructions in our lives—no matter what we call them—are removed, I believe intimacy with God comes.


## Psalm 46:10

Psalm 46:10 (NKJV) gives us a wonderful admonition. *"Be still, and know that I am God..."*

Often times, it is extremely difficult for us to get "still" but it is so much easier when the walls are removed and there's nothing standing in the way of the Presence of God.

The wording "be still" literally means to cease

121

from striving. It means to let go and relax. It means to turn down the volume of the world and listen to the quiet whisper of God. It's getting still and coming into a place of rest. It's entering into His rest and soaking in His Presence. The result is that you will know He is God.

The word "know" is literally an experiential knowledge of God. It's not being still and you'll know about God. It's be still and you will *experientially* know God. You will experience God. You will know the Presence of God.

The living God works from the inside of us outwardly. He begins with our heart first. Normally, we want Him to change our circumstances, all of the outward things we continually face. When our heart is completely His, things begin to change externally.

When His lordship is established in our lives, we can see our circumstances in an entirely different light. Once we come to a place of being "still" in the midst of our circumstances, we recognized God's hand around us.

Intimacy begins when we pursue Him no matter what our circumstances are. He *really* wants us to get to the end of ourselves—and our circumstances—and have nowhere else to turn but to Him. Intimacy will surely follow.

### The 'Martha' Club

Luke 10:38-42 gives us a wonderful example

in the lives of Lazarus' two sisters, Mary and Martha, about the value of true intimacy with God. The sisters lived in the village of Bethany, a suburb two miles east of Jerusalem. It appears Martha is the older sister since verse 38 speaks of her welcoming Jesus "into her house".

> *Now as they were traveling along, He entered a village; and a woman named Martha welcomed Him into her home.*
>
> *She had a sister called Mary, who was seated at the Lord's feet, listening to His word.*
>
> *But as Martha was distracted with all her preparations; and she came up to Him and said, "Lord, do You not care that my sister has left me to do all the serving alone? Then tell her to help me."*
>
> *But the Lord answered and said to her, "Martha, Martha, you are worried and bothered about so many things;*
>
> *but only one thing is necessary, for Mary has chosen the good part, which shall not be taken away from her."*

I was a charter member of the "Martha" Club. I could stay busy all day and half the night just working for the Lord. Yet, I didn't have time to spend alone in His Presence. The Martha "anointing" controlled me.

I'd do all those things we're supposed to do— read the Bible, pray, intercede for others. But I would not take the quality time to seek His face and get into His Presence every day.

Mary chose the better part to sit at the feet of Jesus. That's the best place for all of us. I've told the Lord, "I'm switching clubs. I just want to sit at Your feet and learn from You." I have joined the Mary Club and have caught hold of the Mary "anointing".

I want to challenge you to set a time of day— as your highest priority—to seek the face of God and stay there until you experience His manifest Presence. This is not a time of intercession; it's not a time of seeking His hand ("God give me this" or "God give me that"). Instead, it is a time of seeking His face, His manifest Presence.

People describe His manifest Presence in different ways. To some, it is heat, electricity or shaking. To others, it is lightness, peace or weeping.

Whatever His Presence means in your life, I urge you to experience that place in God every day. It will transform your life. That quest has become the highest priority in my life. I long for His Presence. The more I have the more I want. I have actually become jealous for His Presence.

### A Prayer for Intimacy

I'm often asked, "What do you do in your time of seeking His Presence?" There is not a formula for this. In my life, it varies from time to time but the basic components are as follows:

I go into a private room, lock the door and get

on the floor before the Lord. It doesn't matter whether you sit or lie down. What's most important is the attitude of your heart.

Secondly, I repent of any sin in my life and I receive God's forgiveness.

Thirdly, I worship the Lord in both my native language (English) and in the language of the Holy Spirit.

Fourthly, I do the vital prayer of Romans 6:13 that has transformed my life. (Please see chapter 7).

Then, I begin to recall experiences with the Lord (i.e., healings, miracles, provision) where He has manifested Himself in wonderful ways. This creates more of an expectancy and awareness of His Presence as I relive these times.

I tell the Lord: "God, I want more of You...More of You...More of Your Presence, More of Your fullness in my life. Fill me with more of You..." I may repeat this statement many times as I wait on the Lord and focus on Him. Then, I get quiet and that's when I begin to hear His voice. Often, I begin to have visions and supernatural experiences.

The key here is learning to wait in solitude. I cannot over emphasize the important part of waiting on the Lord until I experience His manifest Presence daily. I don't come out of that private room until I have experienced His Presence.

As you desire to walk in a new level of

intimacy with the Lord, I invite you to join with me in praying this prayer out loud *daily*:

"Lord Jesus, I come now in Your holy Name...unite my heart to fear Your Name and to know Your Presence. Lord, I want greater intimacy with You above everything else. I welcome Your Presence to rule and reign in my life that You may be glorified."

## Chapter 7

# THE PRAYER OF ROMANS 6:13

*"I appeal to you therefore, brethren, and beg of you in view of [all] the mercies of God, to make a decisive dedication of your bodies [presenting all your members and faculties] as a living sacrifice, holy (devoted, consecrated) and well pleasing to God, which is your reasonable (rational, intelligent) service and spiritual worship."*

—Romans 12:1 (Amplified Bible)

In the introduction of his significant book, *Power, Holiness and Evangelism,* Randy Clark, who has spent a number of years as a church pastor and additional years traveling as an international conference speaker, highlights a problem evident in the lives of many churchgoers.  He writes with considerable understanding:

"Is it realistic to even dream of a church that is characterized by unity, power-filled lives, and personal holiness?  I believe so...

"One of the most immediate problems in realizing this dream is that the Church as we know it is not transformed; it is not clean and powerful; and it is not victorious.  It is not full of healed, delivered, self-denying, transformed believers.  Rather, it is often made up of wounded, worn-out warriors.  Many of us in our churches--leaders and members alike--carry weights of buried, unconfessed past sins that we were never meant to carry.  Many of us suffer from unhealed emotional wounds that prevent us from responding to situations, as the Holy Spirit would like to lead us.  Instead, these wounds cause us to respond, consciously or unconsciously, in ways that are influenced or even controlled by our unhealed pain.  Many of us are locked into addictions that are ungodly and unseemly, such as gossip, backbiting, dishonesty, pornography, gluttony, outbursts of anger or hate, uncontrollable sex practices, TV, abiding bitterness, and unforgiveness.  Many persons, even leaders in the Church, live in the realm of the flesh by being touchy, easily offended, controlling, manipulative, greedy, and proud.  Too many are seeking status and man's approval.

"The result is that our witness is hindered, both by the adverse appraisal of those outside the Church and by our own inability to speak the power of God to cleanse, heal, and give victory when our own lives are not cleansed, healed, and victorious.

"Can this be what God intended? Can this be the Church, able to crash through the very gates of hell? It is my conviction that God intends for His sons and daughters to live power-filled, clean, victorious lives that fully honor Him and that fully reflect the indwelling life of His Son. We may not become perfect in this life, but He draws us to move in that direction. He asks us to put aside 'every weight, and the sin which so easily ensnares us' (Hebrews 12:1 NKJV)."

Anyone who has ever pastored a church knows the baffling problem described here by Randy Clark. After pastoring for more than thirty years, I have seen first-hand the problem he so vividly describes in the local church. However, I have also come to see--in my own personal life--that at least part of the solution is a proper application of the living truths from Romans 6:13.

The actual day that the worship leader prayed over me, and my life was so radically changed, was the same day I was introduced by Mike Shea to the liberating truth of Romans 6:13.

> *And do not go on presenting the members of your body to sin as instruments of unrighteousness; but present yourselves to God as those alive from the dead, and your members as instruments of righteousness to God.*

### Understanding Romans 6:13

To experience the liberating power of Romans

6:13, let's begin our study with a review of Romans 6:11-12.

> *Even so consider yourselves to be dead to sin, but alive to God in Christ Jesus.*
> *Therefore do not let sin reign in your mortal body that you should obey its lusts.*

Connecting with the need to be dead to sin, the apostle Paul says *"...I die daily,"* (1 Corinthians 15:31). What is he talking about here? Did he physically die each day?

He's talking about death all right but it's death to sin, selfish desires and his own agenda. He's speaking about dying to the ways of the world, and falling into the traps of the enemy and being pulled away from God's highest and best.

I have often pondered how this anointed man of God could make such a statement. What did he mean? I have looked at Paul's words many times in the light of my experiences. I believe the words *"I die daily"* was his way of saying "no" to the flesh and the fleshly desires of his natural man. He was choosing to live in the realm of the Spirit rather than in the flesh.

When you begin to follow the admonition of Romans 6:13, you're actually having a funeral every day. What happens when a believer dies? There is a separation between the flesh and the spirit. The flesh goes into the ground and the spirit goes directly into the Presence of God.

The apostle Paul tells us being absent from the body is *"to be at home with the Lord,"* (2 Corinthians 5:8)." In His Presence, we can see and hear Him. We can walk and talk with Him. We can actually touch Him.

As we come to a place of allowing ourselves to die daily, we are putting ourselves into a place of becoming alive in the Presence of Jesus Christ. After that first touch from the Lord in Volta Redonda, I died that day and have been dying ever since. I have discovered it's not a one-time experience. It's an ongoing process. I have found, as Heidi Baker says, "God wants to kill us" in order to give us real life...His life. The only way we can truly live is to relinquish control ...to die to our own agenda.

Colossians 3:5 picks up this same theme by stating: *"Therefore consider the members of your earthly body as dead to immorality, impurity, passion, evil desire, and greed, which amounts to idolatry."*

Proverbs 6:16-19 (*author's emphasis*) amplifies our understanding of this sensual nature of man. Let's consider them in the light of our planned funeral.

> *There are six things which the Lord hates, Yes, seven are an abomination to Him:*
> *Haughty **eyes**, a lying **tongue**, and **hands** that shed innocent blood,*
> *A **heart** that devises wicked plans,*

131

**feet** *that run rapidly to evil,*
*A false witness who utters lies, and*
*one who spreads strife among brothers.*

Look at what we're talking about here: eyes, mouth, hands, heart, and feet. When we spend time daily catering to our five natural senses, we can never succeed in the plan of God for our lives. All of us can change *radically* when these senses are yielded over to the Lord. He then becomes our focus and our senses are then opened to receive from Him.

### Praying Romans 6:13

I want to take a few moments now to allow each of us to do business with God because God wants to do business with us. Let's take time to yield the members of our bodies as instruments of righteousness and holiness and not to sin.

Please understand that simply mouthing these words will not bring you the freedom and liberty God wants you to have. Please pray from the depth of your heart as you give your five senses to the Lord.

### Prayer for our Eyes

The Lord speaks about a people who have eyes to see but don't see (Ezekiel 12:2). I lived most of my life in that condition. I just didn't get it. I didn't see what God was doing which is the opposite of what Jesus says about Himself. I wasn't seeing in the realm of the Spirit.

1 John 2:16 cautions us against the *"lust of*

*the eyes"*. This speaks of wandering eyes or eyes that are drawn to all kinds of sensual pleasures. No one can succeed in a spiritual dimension with eyes full of lust.

What are we looking at? Where is the focus of our eyes?

In John 5:19, Jesus said *"Truly, truly, I say to you, the Son can do nothing of Himself, unless it is something He sees the Father doing; for whatever the Father does, these things the Son also does in like manner."*

Jesus was so in tune that He saw exactly what His Father was doing. He was not looking with natural eyes. He was looking with the eyes of the Spirit.

Let's do this...

I want you to give your eyes to the Lord. Tell Him that you want to see with His eyes. (For those involved in any kind of pornography--whether from the Internet, magazines or movies--allow the Holy Spirit to speak to you now).

Tell Him you want to see what He's doing in the earth...

To see things from His perspective....

That you want to behold His beauty....

That He would open the eyes of your spirit

133

and that you might see Him instead of focusing on the things of this world.

"Right now, I give my eyes to You, Lord."

## Prayer for our Ears

Ezekiel 12:2 identifies a rebellious people who have *"ears to hear but do not hear."* That could identify many of us in church this past Sunday--the ones who were sleeping, the ones who were bored or simply the ones looking for an early lunch.

It seems the world is filled up with noise and distractions pulling us in a hundred different directions. The telephone, television, radio, e-mails, faxes--all calling out for you and me.

The problem occurs when God is trying to speak to us and we can't filter out the rest of the noise to hear from heaven. 2 Timothy 4:3-4 speaks about a time when people *"will not endure sound doctrine; but wanting to have their ears tickled...and will turn away their ears from the truth..."*

Truth has the power to liberate you from the problems of life, and to bring you into the favor and blessing of God. Therefore, hearing correctly becomes a vital necessity.

Mark 4:24 is an important Scripture about our hearing. *"Be careful what you are hearing. The measure [of thought and study] you give [to the truth you hear] will be the measure [of virtue and knowledge] that comes back to you—and more [besides] will be given to you who hear,"* (Amplified).

The more we listen to certain things--either good or bad--it becomes a part of our lives. If we discipline ourselves to listen to God's voice, it will produce righteousness, peace and joy. Nothing compares to divine direction in a person's life when that person hears from the Lord.

Now, offer your ears to Him...

We hear so much junk and at times we enjoy hearing some of the stuff that we hear. So, give Him your ears and say, "Lord, just put a filter on my ears to filter out the noise of the world...

"Lord, I ask that I can clearly hear Your voice and that I would have discerning ears...

"Lord, I give You my ears."

### Prayer for our Mouth

James 3:5-12 calls to mind the problem of the tongue; listen to the words of verses 5-6,

> *So also the tongue is a small part of the body, and yet it boasts of great things. See how great a forest is set aflame by such a small fire!*
> *And the tongue is a fire, the very world of iniquity; the tongue is set among our members as that which defiles the entire body, and sets on fire the course of our life, and is set on fire by hell.*

Our tongue affects the course of our life. Think about all the stuff that comes out of our mouths: profanity, lies, half-lies, cruel things, sarcastic things, and hurtful things. Then, there's the great problem with a critical and judgmental spirit. When those kind of words spew out of us, we are not yielded to the Spirit of God.

James 3:9-10 describes how we can do two things with our tongue, *"With it we bless our God and Father, and with it we curse men, who have been made in the likeness of God; from the same mouth come both blessing and cursing. My brethren, these things ought not to be this way."*

Proverbs 18:21 is one of the most significant verses in the Bible about the tongue. *"Death and life are in the power of the tongue, And those who love it will eat its fruit."*

Proverbs 6:2 (NKJV) can be added to the above verse. *"You are snared by the words of your mouth; you are taken by the words of your mouth."*

Now, give Him your mouth...

We are guilty at times of saying a lot of foul things. So, yield your mouth to Him and say, "Lord, I want to speak Your words...

"I want my tongue to be an instrument of righteousness in Jesus' Name...

"I give You my mouth, my tongue, my lips...

"I want to speak what I hear the Spirit saying."

### Prayer for our Nose

2 Corinthians 2:15 tells us something special about ourselves. *"For we are a fragrance of Christ to God among those who are being saved and among those who are perishing."*

What a special place God has literally given us that we have "the fragrance of Christ" attached to our lives. Yet, in many people's lives, there are those dabbling in smells that are unholy. Some are sniffing out things that are unclean and actually taking pleasure in it.

Let's say: "God, I give You my nose...

"I want to be so intimate with You...so close to You...that I can smell Your sweet fragrance, Your perfume.

"Lord, I'm tired of smelling the stench of this world. I want to smell the fragrant incense that surrounds the throne of God...

"Father, this member of my body may seem insignificant to some, but I am yielding it to You...

"Lord, I give You my nose."

### Prayer for our Hands

The apostle Paul brings a challenge to God's

people in 2 Corinthians 6:17 where he combines the thoughts of both Isaiah 52:11 and 2 Samuel 7:14, expressing God's desire for an exclusive, loving relationship with His people.

> *"Therefore, Come out from their midst and be separate," says the Lord. "And do not touch what is unclean; and I will welcome you."*

Stop and think about this Scripture. What are our hands touching that's unclean? What are we doing with our hands that are not of God?

Let's pray and give our hands to God, not for sin, but for righteousness sake...

"God, I give You my hands that they may be used in serving You...

"To reach out to those in need...

"That these hands will be laid on the sick and they will recover...

"Lord, I give You my hands. I want to touch only what You're touching."

### Prayer for our Feet

Proverbs 4:26-27 gives us some cautionary words about our feet. *"Watch the path of your feet, and all your ways will be established. Do not turn to the right nor to the left; turn your foot from evil."*

How often do we wind up walking in paths we had no right to be taking? Many of us have learned the hard way that our feet can take us in a wrong direction.

When Isaiah 52:7 and Romans 10:15 speaks of *"how beautiful are the feet of him who brings good news"*, I believe it speaks of people who are wholly consecrated to the living God. They are people who have given themselves without reservation to the Savior.

Let's say: "God, I give You my feet...

"I'm tired of walking my own way and veering off in this direction and that direction...

"I'm tired of this tangent and following my own agenda...

"Lord, I ask that You order my steps that I might be at the right place where You want me to be at the right time You want me there...

"I'll go where You want me to go.

"Your Word says that a man's steps are ordered or 'established' of the Lord, and I yield my feet to You that this Scripture (Psalm 37:23) may be fulfilled in my life...

"I want to walk in Your ways...

"I want to be right in the center of Your will...

139

"I only want to follow You...to walk with You.

"Lord, I give You my feet."

## Prayer for our Heart

Proverbs 12:20 declares: *"Deceit is in the heart of those who devise evil..."*, and Matthew 15:8 speaks of a people who *"honors Me with their lips, but their heart is far away from Me."*

After thirty years in the Lord' s service, I have painfully discovered that many in His church have hearts wrapped in deceit. Some carry grudges, offenses and unforgiveness, which ultimately control their conduct and shapes their outlook on life.

Jesus Himself calls such people *"hypocrites"* (Matthew 15:7). They may say one thing with their mouth but their heart is not in it. Many are deceived. Their heart is in a totally different place, controlled by inner feelings and emotions that are unworthy of a born again believer.

God wants us to put on a heart of compassion, a pure heart, a heart of love. *"Blessed are the **pure in heart**, for they shall **see** God,"* (Matthew 5:8, *author's emphasis*).

How can we say that we have the Lord's heart when we deal so deceitfully with others? How can we say we truly love His body when we "mouth" platitudes we do not live by.

Pray this: "Lord, I give You my heart...my

broken, wounded, hurting heart.

"I ask that You take my heart of stone, these areas of my heart that have become so hardened against people and even against You...

"Take the hardness away and give me a heart of compassion...

"a heart of love...

"a pure undivided heart...

"a heart for the lost...

"a heart for the needy and the destitute...

"I truly want to experience Your heart, Lord...

"I give You my heart."

### Prayer for our Mind

Let's focus on the mind. Our theme verse here is 2 Corinthians 11:3 (author's emphasis), *"But I am afraid that, as the serpent deceived Eve by his craftiness, your **minds** will be led astray from the simplicity and purity of devotion to Christ."*

How can our minds get off track? The mind is the battlefield. That's where the battle is won or lost in many struggles we face. Thoughts and temptations come to us through the mind. We must learn to handle these mental challenges when they come.

Colossians 3:2 tells us, *"Set your mind on things above, not on the things that are on the earth."*

It is absolutely essential that we set our minds on the Lord Jesus. It is important that we discipline ourselves to set our minds on thinking and mediating on the things of God, on His precious Word and on hearing His direction for our lives.

Romans 8:5-6 encourages us with these words. *"For those who are according to the flesh set their minds on the things of the flesh, but those who are according to the Spirit, the things of the Spirit. For the mind set on the flesh is death, but the mind set on the Spirit is life and peace."*

We can choose what we set our mind on— either the flesh resulting in death or the Spirit resulting in life and peace. It's our choice!

We can learn to take every thought captive to the obedience of Christ (2 Corinthians 10:5). In that place we can develop a renewed mind (Ephesians 4:23).

Let's pause right here and pray this out loud...

"I give my mind to You, Lord...

"I am choosing right now to set my mind on You...

"Lord, I pray to have the mind of Christ operating in my life...

"a renewed mind that I might start thinking like You do...

"Lord, I give You my mind."

## Prayer for Our Whole Person

Pray these words over your life...

"Lord, I give You my whole person--spirit, soul and body...

"God, I give You my whole being...

"I withhold nothing...

"Everything I have is Yours...

"Everything I am is Yours...

"I give it all to You...

"I lay my life on the altar before You...

"I yield myself totally and completely to You...

"Not my will but Your will be done in my life...

"I want More of You in my life. Less will not do...

"More is the cry of my heart...

"Lord, I give You my whole person."

### A Personal Note

I encourage you to pray the prayer of Romans 6:13 *daily* and to yield the members of your body (your five senses) to God.

This is not a formula to gain standing with God or to become more "spiritual" than others. Rather, it is a daily reminder that I am choosing to live according to the Spirit and not the flesh. I choose to die daily as Paul said.

## Chapter 8

# PRAYER OF IMPARTATION!

*"I know that impartation has been the single most important experience in my life to bring about the most fruit in ministry. I have been both the recipient of an important impartation and have been used for important impartations to others who literally have been used to affect nations for the Kingdom of God through the gifts and anointing they received through an impartation."*

--Randy Clark

**K**athi and I have prayed this Prayer of Impartation for thousands of people in countless meetings on several continents. Most of the time, the prayer is made in mass without personally laying hands on anyone.

# OPEN MY EYES, LORD

I have received numerous reports from people whose eyes have been opened. These people have gone to a whole new level in their walk with the Lord as a result of this prayer.

When this prayer has been prayed over God's people, many have had their eyes open to see in the Spirit. More revelations, visions and dreams are common. Others have seen the ministry of angels. Some have had out of body experiences and have been taken up into the Presence of the Lord. At times, it happens right away. For others, it occurs weeks later.

Having one's eyes open to the supernatural is not available only to a select few. It's not just for those in five-fold ministry--apostle, prophet, pastor, teacher, and evangelist. It's for the entire Body of Christ. This impartation will more effectively enable every child of God to carry out the ministry He has placed on each of our lives.

## The Prayer

It is possible that I may never be able to come to your city, state or nation and personally minister to you. However, God works in a supernatural dimension. He can bring an impartation to every person who believes this message and is seeking Him with his or her whole heart.

Now that you have prayed the prayer of Romans 6:13, you are ready for this Prayer of Impartation. Find a quiet place where you can be alone with no distractions. Relax, focus on the Lord and put yourself in neutral. You are seeking the face of God right now, not His hand.

As I pray this Prayer of Impartation, expect to receive a touch from God. Expect the Holy One to manifest Himself to you. Receive this prayer slowly and pause several times to internalize it:

*"Father, I ask You to release Your angels of impartation who would now come into this room and release this impartation...*

*"Come Holy Spirit.*

*"Just as Elisha prayed for Gehazi that his eyes be opened in 2 Kings 6, I pray 'Oh Lord, open his/her eyes that he/she might see in the realm of the Spirit...'*

*"That he/she will see the ministry of angels...*

*"That the scales would be removed from his/her eyes...*

*"Father, open his/her eyes so that he/she can see what You are doing...*

*"Open his/her eyes so that he or she can see things from Your perspective...*

147

# OPEN MY EYES, LORD

*"Lord, open his/her eyes so that he or she can come to a place of higher revelation...*

*"God, I pray you would open his/her eyes to the realm of the unseen...that which is not seen by the natural eye...*

*"I pray that the eyes of his/her spirit would be opened and that his/her eyes would be enlightened...*

*"I pray that he/she will have more visions, more dreams, more revelations and more supernatural encounters with You...*

*"In the Name of the Lord Jesus Christ, I pray. Amen."*

## A Request

Please communicate to us what God begins to do in your life based upon this Prayer of Impartation. Write out your testimony and mail it to Gary Oates Ministries, Inc., P.O. Box 457, Moravian Falls, NC 28654, or email it to info@GaryOates.com.

# PRAYER OF SALVATION

The most important decision you can ever make in life is to receive Jesus Christ as Lord and Savior. You can take that life-changing step by simply praying the following prayer aloud with me:

**Lord Jesus, I ask You to forgive me of my sins and cleanse me from of those things that have kept me in bondage. I surrender to You today. I ask You to come into my heart and be my Lord and Savior. I believe that You are the Son of God and that You were raised from the dead. Thank You for giving me new life as a child of God.**

**In Jesus' Name, Amen.**

*If you've prayed that prayer with me, why don't you take a minute and write me about your decision.*

# About the co-author...

ROBERT PAUL LAMB has worn a number of hats in more than 36 years of ministry including author, pastor, evangelist, prophet, preacher of the Gospel and missionary to the nations. However, he is best known for the 40 books (with some four million copies in print) written on the lives of many of God's great men and women.

He and Gary Oates have been friends and ministerial acquaintances for more than 30 years. Prior to entering the ministry in 1972, he had spent most of his adult life in public relations and newspaper work. He and his family live in the foothills of northwestern North Carolina.

# Ministry Resources
## by
# *Gary Oates*

## CD's and DVD's

**MP3 now available for immediate download**
**Various conference CD & DVD sets available**

## Quantity discounts available for books!

These and other titles available at:

www.GaryOates.com, or phone 336-667-2333

For book/tape/video orders,
please contact:

## Open Heaven Publications
*an outreach of Gary Oates Ministries, Inc.*
P.O. Box 457/Moravian Falls, NC 28654 USA
336-667-2333

For more information, visit our website:
www.GaryOates.com